Dar

How To Use Neuro-linguistic Programming For Self Mastery, Getting What You Want, Mastering Others And To Gain An Advantage Over Anyone

By Michael Pace

Copyright 2015 by Michael Pace

Published by Make Profits Easy LLC

Profitsdaily123@aol.com

facebook.com/MakeProfitsEasy

Table of Contents

Chapter 1 - Introduction 4

Chapter 2 - The Foundations of Dark NLP 16

Chapter 3 - Why is NLP so Notoriously Controversial? 41

Chapter 4 - Master Yourself before You Master Others 55

Chapter 5 - Take Control of Others 77

Chapter 6 - Take Control of the Past, Present and Future 92

Chapter 7 - Take What You Want Without Apology 115

Chapter 8 - Understand How to Exploit Your Hidden Advantage 138

Chapter 9 - Powerful Dark Hypnotic Seduction 161

Chapter 10 - Learn from the Masters of NLP .. 183

Chapter 11 - Inaction Equals Death 198

Chapter 1 - Introduction

<u>Dark NLP Secrets</u>

This book contains a lethal combination of principles and ideas. The book deals not only with the controversial school of personal influence known as NLP, but combines this with the most secretive aspects of psychology to form a new system known as Dark NLP. This book is your complete guide to the principles that form the basis of Dark NLP, as well as devastatingly effective ways to put them to work for you in your life. By reading this book's contents in its entirety and vowing to put it to work in your life, you will gain a significant advantage over your rivals in many areas.

The unique power of this book is its ability to distill complex psychological principles into a simple explanation that anyone can understand. It takes these ideas and filters them through systems of dark thought such as Machiavellianism and covert manipulation. After the principles have been thoroughly explained and illustrated with applied examples, they are further simplified into a series of actionable steps. By following these steps, anyone is able to apply the ideas within the chapter to their life.

The book is written in a way that allows each chapter to build on the one before it. The ideas from previous chapters may be referenced and reused in new ways in later chapters. For this reason it is intended that the reader follow the book in its presented order. After you have read the work in order once, you will be able to dip in and out of chapters as needed. Skipping chapters initially, however, will lead to knowledge gaps making your understanding of Dark NLP incomplete.

Your Secret Life Advantage

Due to the fact that the psychological principles upon which Dark NLP is based are universal, you will soon see that the ideas within this book will give you an advantage in almost any area of your life to which they are applied. Your career, romantic life, friendships and even casual interactions will all benefit from the tactics you learn. To inspire you to take action and continue reading this book, you will now get a brief taste of how your life will benefit from Dark NLP.

Imagine a career in which you are not only respected and listened to, but able to influence the outcome of any interaction to your direct advantage. Imagine a romantic life in which you not only had no fear of interacting with new people, but knew precisely what to say, and what to do around them at any stage of your relationship. Imagine the freedom to interact with anyone, for any duration, knowing you will be able to captivate that person completely.

You should have a complete understanding of what you wish to get out of the experience before delving deeper into this book. Think about how your goals relate to your values. For example, do you want to gain a greater sense of freedom? Do you want to feel more significance? Do you want to add a greater sense of variety into your life? Only when you understand how the experience of reading, acting on the book's contents will add to your life values, will you have the desire and motivation to take powerful enough action on what you read.

The business world thrives on competitive advantage. This concept can be explained as an organization's ability to combine resources and experiences in order to do something unique or something better than anyone else can do it. Competitive advantage can also be applied to individuals as the idea of having a skill or ability that those they interact with do not. This book will provide you with exactly that - a secret skill set that those around you do not possess. Think of the confidence that will come from taking action on what you read.

Prepare Yourself

Hopefully by this point you are at least intrigued about the possibility of what Dark NLP will mean in your life when you apply it diligently. You will first learn the basic ideas of NLP itself including the principles behind it and some of the main ways in which it is applied. This foundation is essential in order to understand how it can be filtered through the lens of dark psychology for a uniquely powerful system of influence.

You will then be provided with a thorough background of how NLP has proven to be such a powerful and controversial force over the years. Some of the darkest and most powerful uses of NLP will be shown to you in the form of real life stories based on corrupt and shocking motivations. The ideas behind each story will then be extracted and summarized as a series of Dark NLP principles that underpin the rest of the book.

The book then explains the importance of using NLP to first master yourself before using it to influence others. You will be shown exactly how to use NLP to understand your deepest hopes, fears and motivations, as well as how to leverage them through NLP. You will also be shown how NLP can change your habits, motivate you and eradicate phobia and self-doubt from your life once and for all.

The book then delves into its most controversial chapter - using Dark NLP to directly influence others. You will be shown exactly how to figure out a person's unique 'blueprint' - the exact system of how they think and the ways in which it can be turned against them to make them do precisely what you want. It is vital that you treat every person you interact with as a unique target. Everyone has a unique system of weaknesses. You will be shown exactly how to identify and exploit these.

You will also be shown two powerful ways of understanding and influencing a person, including how to read their eye movements to understand what they are thinking and if it is truthful, as well as how to read their language to understand their deepest thoughts. By using these two things in combination, you will effectively have the ability to read and take control of another person's mind.

The concepts of NLP will then be taken to another level entirely as you are shown how to read, interpret and match a person's physical body language to influence and control how they feel. By mirroring a person's physicality they will feel a deep sense of rapport with you that they are not able to attribute to your manipulation. You will then be shown how to subtly lead the interaction and check their compliance through their mirroring of your body language.

After you have a thorough understanding of how NLP can be used to take control of both yourself and others, you will be shown how to use it to interpret the world around you. You will learn how to see the world through the lens of NLP principles and how doing so liberates you from the shackles of conventional thought. NLP will prove to be effective in understanding your life in all three dimensions of time - past, present and future. You will begin to understand your past failures as lessons that can be learned from, set goals that are tied to your present values and powerfully envision your future through the principles of Dark NLP.

Direct tactics and techniques that can be used to get what you want out of life will then be revealed. You will learn reinforcement techniques which can be used to ensure you stay on a path of action tied to your values. You will be given a simple formula of how to create profoundly powerful mantras which can be used as part of a routine for the morning or evening to reinforce your values and path of action. You will then be given specific techniques and tactics, essentially applied Dark NLP, which are used to carry out different objectives.

The deep advantage that comes from understanding and applying Dark NLP will then be explained. The advantage will be applied to a variety of scenarios, showing exactly how to use Dark NLP in a strategic way at any given time. Using Dark NLP in this broadly strategic way is more powerful than simply using its ideas in isolation. Various strategies and the risks and rewards they offer you will be explained in a way which makes it easy to take significant levels of powerful action.

One of the most controversial areas of NLP will then be described in detail - how to use NLP in your pursuit of romantic seduction. This is one of the most polarizing aspects of NLP and the tradition of using it to gain influence over a romantic target will be explained in great detail. You will be given a breakdown of the specific Dark NLP techniques that are used within the romantic sphere of life. You can use these either as a warning of what to avoid, or as a system to use for your own means.

In order to gain deeper insight into the practical applications of NLP you will be given a series of case studies into the most accomplished practitioners of the discipline. You will not only be taught their accomplishments but also given ways of applying their techniques in your own life. The power of this section is it distills the wisdom of the greatest users of NLP in a way that saves you years of study. The book shares insight into the NLP concept of modeling and how it can be used to understand the life lessons and behaviors of anyone and apply them to your own life.

<u>Do or Die</u>

Did you know that the number of people who finish a book requiring action to be taken is as low as 20%? Most people don't even read beyond the first chapter. This is your chance - your do or die moment. You have to make a decision. You can either join the lazy majority who walk through life in a daydream or the small minority of people who seek to take direct control of their lives. You can seize this chance to learn darkly powerful techniques that will give you control of life and all its areas, or you can stay within your comfort zone and passively take what life gives you.

The future ahead of us is only going to be a more cutthroat and competitive place than ever before. There is a significant chance that further world economic turmoil will result in the competition for jobs becoming fiercer than ever before. This book will give you the chance to stand out in this new, brutal reality and ensure that you always are equipped to deal with the changing landscape of life. We also live in a world of high divorce rates fueled by people so scared of being alone they jump into marriage without thinking it through. By knowing the romantic applications of this book you will ensure yourself a life of romantic abundance and satisfaction.

By taking the first step on this journey into the world of Dark NLP you are accepting that the path ahead may shock and surprise you at times. You are agreeing to see the world as it really is without any of the naive assumptions of mainstream thought. If you think human beings are moral and kind, be prepared to be appalled. You will be given a no-holds-barred look into the depths of just how self-serving and desperate people truly are.

In return for your commitment and willingness to be shocked, you will receive massive rewards. You will gain the most powerful insight possible into yourself and into others. You will never again feel directionless or powerless in life, and until your dying day you will have a rock solid path tied into your deepest values. So, what will it be? A life of abundance and freedom, or a comfortable life of disappointment and scarcity?

The choice is yours. But choose wisely - if you refuse to be the hunter, you will inevitably become the hunted.

Chapter 2 - The Foundations of Dark NLP

The Origins of Dark NLP

To understand Dark NLP on a theoretical level, it is first necessary to understand the ideas of NLP upon which it is based. NLP began when two individuals, Bandler and Grinder, developed a set of ideas into human behavior and how it could be influenced that came to be known as neuro-linguistic programming, more commonly known as NLP. At first, the techniques were fairly unknown, but received wider exposure through the years through the work of superstars such as Tony Robbins and Derren Brown. Although more people than ever before have heard of NLP, very few know how to actually apply it.

The basic concepts of NLP came from the modeling of human behavior combined with linguistic principles taken from academics such as Noam Chomsky. These two central influences are combined into a set of formal principles into the motivations of humans and how these can be influenced and modeled. One of the founders of NLP has summarized its area of focus as formalizing the concepts and principles which drive human behavior.

NLP has three main areas through which its ideas are filtered - subjectivity, consciousness and learning. NLP teaches that there is no absolute, objective understanding of the world around us, yet instead every individual forms their own personal picture of the world which consists of the data taken in through the five senses as well as the language the person learns to attach to their sensory data. It is theorized that this combination of sensory input and descriptive language eventually leads to behaviors that are either effective according to our subjective map of the world, or maladaptive and harmful to our own aims and pursuits.

One area in which NLP is relatively in agreement with mainstream psychology is its understanding of the human mind as having both a conscious and an unconscious dimension. Much of the teaching of NLP is predicated upon the belief that a lot of influence occurs at the subconscious level of human thought. People are vulnerable to being manipulated in ways they are not able to perceive.

NLP sees people as behaving according to three key aspects - the 'what', the 'how' and the 'why'. The 'what' focuses on the external behavior and physiology a person exhibits in a given situation, the 'how' deals with the internal thinking patterns the person has that govern their pattern of decision making, and the 'why' deals with the supporting beliefs, assumptions and values that point a person in one direction rather than another.

If you are able to understand the aforementioned three aspects then you are able to effectively model the complete reality of someone else's behavior. It should be stressed that it is the internal process that is being copied which leads to the external behavior, rather than just crudely mimicking the external behavior alone. Without the accompanying internal dimensions, the behavior is likely to come off as insincere and phony.

NLP advocates going beyond passively accepting the various factors that compromise a person's behavior. Instead, it advocates actively exploring and manipulating the variables at hand in order to understand the relationship between each, and which are essential to achieve the desired result. There is a clear contrast between the NLP model of understanding behaviors and the traditional view. Traditionally, people acquire a new behavior by acquiring one piece of a skill at a time, until they add up to form the entire behavior. NLP instead focuses on doing things the opposite way, meaning the person is initially presented with all of the components of a behavior at once, and then proceeds to subtract various parts until they are left with only the essential aspects.

This process of simplifying behaviors and reducing them to only their crucial aspects is similar to business processes which aim to map out a series of steps and identify which are essential and which are not. In this sense, the process of refining behaviors through the application of NLP can be seen as a means of ensuring personal efficiency.

NLP also concerns itself with the question of finding the difference between two types of people within any given field - those that succeed and those who do not. Success modeling seeks to find exactly what previously successful people did in contrast from someone who failed in the same area of life. Did they think about the problem differently? Did they perceive decisions differently? Was there some behavioral habit that helped to make the difference to their results?

The main outlook of NLP can therefore be summarized as identifying and simplifying the factors that lead to success in a given situation as a simple process model. When this model has been identified and simplified it can be applied to gain drastic results in a short period of time. This is because the years of experience that have lead to successful people doing things a certain way can be quickly and painlessly adopted by anyone willing.

This above understanding of NLP is essential to understanding Dark NLP but it is only half of the equation. Equally important is the understanding of the dark psychological principles through which the traditional NLP outlook on human behavior is filtered. This unique system is able to combine the unfiltered truth of dark psychological insight with the manipulative efficiency of NLP to make a truly unique model of understanding. So what are the main dark psychological concepts which bear influence upon NLP?

One of the key ideas informing Dark NLP is that human beings lack any concrete identity and are therefore susceptible to the influence of others, for better or for worse. Traditional NLP takes this understanding of identity as being fluid and uses it as a basis for therapists to help people overcome the major roadblocks that are holding them back in life. According to Dark NLP, on the other hand, this fluidity of identity means that a person can be manipulated into behaving according to the will of others. This potential for malicious influence is evidenced by the people who fall under the spell of dark forces such as cults or extreme ideologies.

Dark psychology also understands that human beings are less in control of their own will than they tend to believe. When asked, the majority of people will report being almost entirely in control of their own thought processes, and state that they would not obey an instruction that goes against their own free will. One classic experiment in psychology that has directly influenced the concepts of dark psychology shatters this misconception. In the famous Milgram experiment, volunteers were told to administer electric shocks who gave a wrong answer during a learning test. The majority of those being told to administer the shocks continued to do so even when they could hear the supposed screams of the person being punished. This experiment shows that people have an inherent obedience to authority and less free will than they tend to assume. Similarly, the famous Zimbardo experiment offers an insight into another aspect that underpins dark psychology, which is the willingness of human beings to assume behaviors based upon their role in any given situation. In Zimbardo's experiment, participants were divided at random into either prison guards or prisoners. Those who received the role of prison guard became increasingly willing to carry out acts of cruelty and abuses of power as the experiment went on.

When taken together, Milgram and Zimbardo's experiments offer the following concepts, which are core principles behind dark psychology - people can be easily led and behaviors can be influenced in numerous ways. This realization is too disturbing for most people so they choose not to believe it, despite the evidence that shows it to be true. The minority of people who are willing to exploit these ideas are therefore uniquely situated to take advantage of the naive masses for their own ends.

Another key idea behind dark psychology is that of 'priming'. Priming states that people can be influenced by a variety of factors outside of their perception into behaving in a certain way. For example, the choice of language that is used when speaking to a person has been shown to influence the speed at which they move afterwards. Furthermore, words that sound similar to other words can be used to subliminally plant ideas into a person's mind without them being aware that any such thing has taken place. This is one of the techniques used by hypnotists such as Derren Brown to make people do things without understanding why.

Dark psychology also exploits the tendency of human beings to be susceptible to a majority opinion, even when this influence goes against their own rationality and perception. This was evidenced by a series of experiments by researcher Asch, who found that subjects changed their own ideas about when influenced by a group majority. This concept of majority influence is often used by groups with extremist ideologies to brainwash those they wish to influence. When a person is surrounded by people espousing certain views and opinions, they end up not only genuinely believing what they have heard, but feeling as if they have done so under their own free will.

A Willingness to Accept

As the best psychological researchers will tell you, a key part of successful research is being able to accept what the evidence shows you, rather than seeking to confirm preconceived theories. This concept applies to your individual pursuit of Dark NLP as well, since you have to be willing to accept that what works, works. It may not look the way you hoped and you may not like what it tells you about people.

The willingness to accept also extends to the times you will be required to look at yourself and the choices you have made. There is no point in shying away from seeing things as brutally honestly as possible. This book will repeatedly emphasize the need to move away from judging yourself and instead always seeking to learn from yourself. The requirement to look inward with total honesty and accept what you see is simultaneously the hardest and most impactful aspect of your Dark NLP progress. It is an ability which will allow you to move through life with a solid, unflinching grounding in reality. When you learn to avoid fearing the truth, you come to realize that nothing in life need faze you anymore.

<u>Find Your Reasons</u>

No one can tell you what the process of learning, implementing and mastering the techniques of Dark NLP will mean for you. If you have the willpower to pay attention to the teachings of this book and interpret what they mean for your life, then you need to have a firm motivation for acting. It is important to approach this personal motivation from two angles - the things in life you are moving away from, and the things in life you are moving toward.

Some examples of the things in life you may be moving away from by using Dark NLP include feeling powerless in social situations, frustration and lack of options in your romantic life, feelings directionless and meandering through life, and doubts about your ability to achieve the life of your dreams.

Some of the things you may be seeking to move towards by studying Dark NLP include a greater sense of power, a clearer sense of your values and drives in life, a means of figuring out the people around you and the things that cause them to behave the way they do, and a general sense of power and control in any situation life puts you in.

It is important to have a clear sense of the most important aspects you are moving away from and moving toward. Having just one or the other is not enough. There are times when you will feel more motivated by the things you are seeking to escape, and other times when you will be more encouraged to pursue a desired future state of affairs. By having a firm sense of both objectives, you are helping to ensure that your motivation remains present at all times.

There is no such thing as a worthy or unworthy aim for using Dark NLP since whatever matters to you is sufficient. Your aims and intentions don't have to meet any external standard - as long as they mean something to you, they will be sufficiently motivational to boost your chances of taking action and succeeding in this area of life.

There is no escaping the fact that there will be tests to your resolve as you attempt to learn, implement and improve this new skill set. You will have times where your instinct is to retreat into your old way of doing things as it is comfortable and familiar to you. By learning to reframe times such as these as an inevitable and important part of your development, you will come to embrace rather than fear them.

Kill These Illusions

In order to take on board act upon the ideas of Dark NLP, it is first essential to rid yourself of many misconceptions and limiting beliefs you may have. A limiting belief, in this context, is any viewpoint you have which holds you back from applying the ideas of Dark NLP to your own life. So what are some of the most common misconceptions you may have and how do you overcome them?

One of the most common problems holding people back from taking a greater amount of influence over their life is the belief that it is somehow immoral or wrong to do so. This often stems from the environment in which a person has grown up. If you have grown up in a home where things are done very passively, and being assertive is frowned upon, you may initially find it difficult to begin taking a greater degree of control over your own life. You can overcome this misconception by continually reminding yourself of both the frustrations that you are currently experiencing in life as a result of not being assertive, and the many benefits and good feelings you will experience after taking control of the various parts of your life where you are currently unsatisfied.

You may also have the mistaken understanding that a person's behavior is equivalent to their identity. For example, you might identify yourself as a shy person, rather than a person who is currently exhibiting shy behaviors. This may sound like an unimportant distinction, but in reality it is anything but. When someone makes their behaviors equivalent to their identity, it makes the behaviors far harder to either remove or change. This is because to do so, such a person would feel as if they were betraying their core identity. If, on the other hand, a person is able to recognize that their behaviors do not define them, and that by changing their behaviors they are not betraying their sense of self, then it is easier to make radical changes within such a person's life.

Many people also have a misconception about the value of various resources in life. For example, many people think that money is the ultimate objective in life, whereas it should instead be viewed as a tool that can be used to gain other things such as freedom and security. A key understanding that people must attain in their pursuit of Dark NLP prowess is that the only truly finite resource is time. We can always make more money but we can never recover even a second of our lives. For this reason, those who understand the ideas of Dark NLP are focused on being ruthless and efficient as they understand that time is the only thing they will never get back.

Seeing the path of your life as fixed or immovable is another common obstacle people have when attempting to learn and apply Dark NLP. This often stems from a belief in fate or destiny. Dark NLP, on the other hand, states that nothing is set in stone and everything is subject to a range of influences in life. If you believe in destiny or fate, it is important to try to shift your understanding in favor of the view that we can change and alter the events of our life. Without this belief, your efforts to exert influence will be empty and ineffectual. We are unable to influence ourselves, or those around us, until we truly believe that we are able to.

<u>The Red Pill</u>

Now that we know the limiting beliefs and false outlooks, that hold us back, it is important to explore the correct beliefs and viewpoints that are essential to effectively use NLP.

The most important understanding to have is that no one has a fixed identity, and everything and everyone is subject to a range of influences. For some people, this belief is easier to adopt than for others. It can be upsetting, as it means that we are in less control than we may have assumed, but also liberating, as it means we are always free to reinvent ourselves at any stage in our life.

It is also important to fully embrace the fact that conventional morality is an illusion and people are in fact willing to perform acts that go against the prevailing morality of their culture if it means they will personally benefit from doing so. This has been emphasized in two ways; firstly, through theoretical works such as those of Machiavelli, and secondly, through scientific experiments such as those of Zimbardo.

The next required is the understanding that morality is always relative and no absolute standards exist. Although there are many common prohibitions across various different cultures, there is no universal standard of morality. Indeed, all similarities can be explained by the fact that they are in accordance with Darwin's theory of evolution. If something is useful for survival of the species then it tends to be incorporated into the moral norms of the time.

It is also important to realize that Dark NLP will often encourage you, or at least open your mind to the possibility of operating in a way that is contrary to the teachings of religion and other forms of conventional social influence. One example of this commonly occurring conflict is the teaching of NLP to master yourself and then use this to control others going directly against the Christian teaching that it is praiseworthy to be meek. Upon rational examination, it becomes clear that the Christian teaching is intended to act as a form of social control, whereas the Dark NLP teaching is intended to empower people to shamelessly pursue whatever they want out of life. The latter teaching is intended to benefit the individual directly, whereas the former teaching is intended to make people passive and therefore easy to control.

There is also no escaping the fact that Dark NLP will teach you to go against the prevalent social view that people work well together and interactions should be viewed as collaborative opportunities. Instead, this book teaches that every interaction should be viewed as a zero sum, adversarial encounter in which one party wins and the other loses. You should always seek to gain the upper hand and win the struggle for power in any given encounter. The majority of the time, you will be able to do this with very little effort as the other party will now be viewing the encounter as a power struggle. The small percentage of the time that they are, you will have the tactics and techniques to beat them every time.

Dark NLP also goes against the prevailing social norm by teaching that a monogamous approach to relationships is far from the only way. This book does not suggest that monogamy is bad, only that it is one option of many. People should not feel pressured into adopting a monogamous lifestyle just because it happens to be the social norm of the time. A monogamous lifestyle should be chosen from an understanding of abundance in which a person is aware they have a multitude of options. Counter intuitively, this increases the chance of a successful relationship as both parties feel they have chose the other, rather than being pressured into a relationship out of neediness.

The truth of Dark NLP can be summed up as a willingness to accept that acting in self-interest is not immoral. Indeed, you will eventually come to see that morality is entirely fluid and therefore cannot be the basis upon which you make your decisions. Instead, it is always better to make a decision based on self-interest alone. This is the only way to consistently guarantee that the outcome to your choices will work in your favor.

Predator or Prey

Next, a variety of applied examples will show how putting into practice the ideas of Dark NLP will help you to have a clear advantage in a number of different situations. This is highlighted through the concept of predator or prey - namely that in any given social interaction there is one person who is acting and one person who is being acted upon. This section of the chapter shows the importance of being the active party and teaches you how to achieve this in a variety of different areas of life.

Imagine for example that you are undergoing an appraisal as part of your ongoing professional assessment. In this situation there are two ways in which you can either take decisive action or risk being acted upon - in the appraisal of your performance over the previous year, and in the setting of targets for your upcoming year. We will now show how each aspect greatly benefits from your taking control of it through the use of Dark NLP tactics.

When your performance over the previous year is being discussed, you have the choice of either passively accepting the way in which the assessor describes the facts, or of representing the information in a way that highlights your own achievements and shows your performance in a good light. This is known as reframing. The importance of reframing and the ways in which it can benefit you will now be explored in greater depth.

Imagine, for example, during the appraisal of your previous year the assessor mentions you were part of a successful project team. You can either passively accept this description, or you can actively choose to reframe it to a way in which your own personal efforts are more prominent. For example, you might choose to say "Yes, I was the most productive member, statistically, of that project team." Let's analyze why this is effective. You have agreed with the assessor and therefore made them feel at ease with you, but you have done so in a way that subtly has shown off what you did in particular.

It is also important to use the ideas of Dark NLP when setting goals for the upcoming work year. During most annual appraisals the setting of goals is a compulsory part of the process. Like anything that is compulsory, you have the choice of either passively waiting to hear what has been determined for you by others, or of attempting to actively influence the situation. Often, if you suggest a few goals which you have determined beforehand, the assessor will be so impressed with your proactivity that they will agree to what you have suggested. So what type of goals should you suggest?

It is important to think of goals which resonate with your core values. This will prove to be a powerful leverage and motivation in pursuing your workplace goals even when your situational motivation levels fluctuate. You should also ensure that the goals you suggest are achievable. You might be tempted to suggest huge goals that sound impressive to the assessor, but in the long run this will only harm if you if you are unable to deliver on what you have proposed. You should therefore aim to strike a balance between goals which will sound ambitious enough, but that you are also capable of realistically achieving.

It is also important to keep this idea of predator or prey in mind during your interaction within the romantic sphere of life. It is a sad fact that many people out there are only seeking to exploit others through their interactions with them, under the guise of seeking romance. By filtering this truth through the lens of our 'predator or prey' filter we can see that such people are trying to make us the prey in the situation. By being wary of the concept of prey, you are always guarded against naively slipping into the trap set by another.

You can also keep the idea of predator or prey in mind when making decisions as a consumer. There is perhaps no more effective tool that has ever existed than the advertising industry in making large numbers of people into prey under the control and influence of others. In any given situation where you are attempting to make a purchase, it is important to calmly and rationally analyze your reasons for wanting to do so. You should be sure that the reason you wish to spend money is based upon a logical need rather than an emotional response to marketing messages. You should also be wary of falling into psychologically tempting practices such as pricing discounts which tempt you into buying something you wouldn't otherwise consider.

Chapter 3 - Why is NLP so Notoriously Controversial?

You will now receive full access into the world of Dark NLP. It is important to remember that the principles and techniques of this school of thought are in direct contradiction to mainstream morality and social norms, so you should be prepared to have your preconceptions challenged. This chapter will begin with a number of real life examples into how the power of NLP can change lives for better or for worse. We will then explore some of the darkest and most controversial uses of NLP that have ever been devised. The chapter will conclude with a look at the range of controversies centering around NLP that have taken place over the years.

By exploring the controversies that NLP has generated, you will gain a range of insights. First, you will see that often NLP is criticized not for the actual content it contains but for its ability to challenge widely held viewpoints. Anything that goes against the grain of popular thought is bound to court controversy, regardless of what it teaches. You will also gain insight into the power of NLP to grant additional influence to absolutely anyone. Anything that has the potential to disrupt the established social order is seen as controversial and NLP is no exception.

The Power of NLP - Real Life Examples

Next, we will look at a range of insights into the power that NLP has to influence lives. This section does not seek to take a moral stance on the NLP examples that are provided, rather seeks only to use them to show the immense power of NLP when used effectively. The ideas from each story will be extracted and explained so that you understand exactly what has taken place in each of the examples and why the results have occurred.

One powerful example of NLP is how it can cure people of addictions that negatively impact their life. One such story is of a man who visited an NLP therapist complaining of his inability to give up smoking cigarettes. Even though he had experienced bad health effects as the result of his habit and was spending a lot of money on three packs a day, he had been unable to find the motivation to give up.

The NLP therapist was able to use a series of envisioning techniques to replace the view that the man had of cigarettes. Instead of seeing them as a guilty pleasure, the man swapped his imagery of cigarettes with that of death and bad health. As a result of manipulating his internal viewpoint, the man no longer desired cigarettes and was able to quit.

Another testament to the power of NLP stems from the world of business. One high-ranking female executive in a European division of a technology company was summoned to a meeting in America with an intimidating executive. Although she was well respected within her division of the company, she had achieved this by being likeable and genuinely supportive of those she worked with. She did not have a high level of assertion and was therefore fearful of the meeting in America.

The woman decided to visit an NLP teacher in order to learn some ways by which she could feel more comfortable and confident about the meeting in America. She was taught an NLP technique known as anchoring in which she was able to link an emotion to a physical trigger. In this case, she was taught to think back through her past to a time when she felt totally confident and in control of what was taking place. She was able to do this. She was then instructed to link this feeling to a ball of colored light. She was then told to move this colored light onto the floor in front of her and use it to draw a circle around her. This gave the woman an immense feeling of total security and confidence within the boundaries of the circle.

When it came time for the woman's meeting in America, she was able to draw upon this technique and use it to get rid of her fears about interacting with the executive. She was able to calmly and collectedly deal with the situation at hand. It turns out she was not even being criticized or disciplined and they merely wanted to discuss strategy with her. Because of her NLP training, however, she was able to avoid experiencing the negative impact of stress and worry.

Some of the most controversial but effective users of NLP have used it in their pursuit of romance. There are several schools of thought dedicated entirely to teaching seduction based upon the ideas of NLP and there is an entire chapter later in this book on that very topic. For now, a brief insight will be provided into how effective this can be.

One of the most well known teachers of NLP runs seminars in which men learn how to use NLP based methods to induce good feelings in members of the opposite sex and increase their chances of having a successful romantic encounter. The methods revolve around somewhat esoteric ideas such as generating a positive internal state which can then be passed on to the other person through the law of state transference. The ideas behind this, and the ways of carrying it out, are fully detailed in the seduction chapter later in this book.

The examples provided so far are some of the more positive and acceptable uses of NLP in people's lives. This chapter's next section will show how these ideas can be reimagined in a dark way which draws upon human weakness to manipulate and covertly influence others. It should be noted that ideas such as these exist on the fringe of the NLP community - they are not widely accepted or even known about. They are the dark secrets of the NLP world which are about to be widely revealed for the very first time.

The Darkest Real World NLP Examples

One dark area of application for NLP has been within the schools of seduction based around this area of influence. While the majority of men and women using the ideas behind NLP to help their chances of success in the dating world do so in a mainstream and acceptable way, a few fringe figures have devoted themselves to learning darkly devastating applications for NLP teachings. You are advised to read on with caution as the following ideas are deadly if in the wrong hands.

Patterns are a common way of referring to the dark NLP techniques that are used for seduction purposes. A series of patterns gained notoriety within the seduction community and became to be known as the banned patterns. They earned this name due to the fact they were deemed far too dark and amoral for the community to accept. Due to their notoriety, they have often been sought out by the community, but are hard to find. They are presented here in full.

One such pattern is known as 'the shadow and the rising sun.' It is widely banned within the seduction community due to the fact that it draws upon the ideas found in Jungian psychology to unlock a woman's dark side, the hidden shadow of her personality.

This is achieved by the seducer beginning to talk about the idea of contrasts. He focused on talking about contrasting imagery that is able to evoke the idea of darkness such as light and dark, day and night and yin and yang. He talks about how a darkside is an essential part of life and without one, nothing is meaningful. He then begins to talk about how everyone has a darkside. This can be seen as the idea of a rising sun which casts a shadow and changes the perspective on everything. The seducer then invites the target to step into her dark side and view the world through its lens. This is intended to put the target into a susceptible state where they behave in a way which they otherwise would not.

Another technique that is often used in conjunction with the above technique is known as the hospital pattern. In this pattern, the seducer fluctuates his target's emotional state between extreme feelings of pleasure and extreme feelings of pain. This rapid change of emotional states, which swing back and forth multiple times, are intended to leave the target feeling emotionally unstable and therefore susceptible to influence. When the target is in this susceptible state, the seducer is able to anchor the target's perception of pleasure to himself, and perception of pain to something other than himself. By doing this, the seducer is able to ensure that the target feels immense pleasure associated with the seducer, who can trigger these feelings on demand.

Another dark usage of NLP in the pursuit of seduction is something known as a pattern interrupt. This is where the seducer uses Dark NLP to stop his target from doing something he does not want and to reduce her rationality and defense mechanisms. For example, if the target begins to list logical reasons why she should not be with the seducer, the seducer may ask her something totally unrelated like "What's your favorite color?" By doing this, the seducer disrupts the target's thought process and therefore defense mechanisms. This stops the target from falling into their habitual patterns.

NLP has also been used in a dark way to make people question which of their memories are real and which are fabricated. There is a technique in which the target is put into a state of relaxation that is often likened to being somewhere between awake and asleep. In this state, the target is deeply suggestible. The target is guided back through their memories until the user of Dark NLP finds a memory they wish to disrupt. They then ask a series of questions which are intended to make the target doubt if the memory ever actually occurred or if they imagined it. This can be used to disrupt the target's feeling of identity and make them question the beliefs and values they have about who they are. This is often the first step in the process of brainwashing someone into having a new identity.

A similar technique can be used to implant false memories into a target's mind which are perceived as real. Just as in the last technique, the target is put into a state of deep relaxation, in which they become susceptible to influence. They are then led back through their memories. At the appropriate point, the target is asked a series of leading questions into remembering something that didn't happen. This often begins with a real memory, and then the target will be asked things such as "Then do you remember when x happened?" and '"How did you feel when x happened?" By framing the question in the latter way, the target's brain focuses on recalling an emotional response. Since the fact the event has taken place is presented as a statement, the brain assumed it to be true. This is used to make people remember things that have never happened to them, such as when cults cause victims to imagine they have suffered abuse from their parents that never actually took place. This is often used to separate a target from their environment.

The Controversy of NLP

NLP has proven to be one of the most controversial subsets of psychology. We will now explore a range of the controversies that NLP has generated and explore exactly why this discipline is perceived as so troubling and controversial by the mainstream. In doing this, the power of NLP will be clearly illustrated and shown in a way which highlights how far outside the boundaries of mainstream thought NLP, and in particular Dark NLP, really is.

Some of the earliest criticisms of NLP came from within the mainstream psychology profession. Traditional therapists and psychologists stated that NLP was dangerous as it took shortcuts to achieve results that were only possible after prolonged, traditional therapy. The psychologists stated that taking these shortcuts meant that people were not truly healed; rather they just learned to bury their traumas even deeper. The NLP world hit back and stated that the psychology profession was just worried as their slow results were becoming less and less acceptable to people. The fight for legitimacy is something that has coexisted with NLP since its initial days.

One controversy surrounding NLP is the fact that it is seen as encouraging immoral behavior. Because NLP teaches people how to deeply understand and influence others, it is seen as encouraging people to act in ways which will be detrimental and selfish. NLP teachers have hit back and said it is unfair to single out NLP for this criticism. Almost any school of thought can be used for good or for bad, and it is not the fault of anyone but the individual using techniques for immoral purposes.

Many people, particularly within feminist circles, have criticized the use of NLP for seduction. They state that it removes the element of choice and makes people do things they would not normally agree to. The counter argument to this perspective is that NLP can be used to genuinely enhance a romantic encounter and help people feel a greater range of positive emotion. The majority of people using NLP for romantic purposes do so with good intentions. The few individuals who do not are to blame for any blameworthy uses, not the ideas themselves.

The model of teaching NLP has also been criticized over the years. It has been alleged that the environment in which NLP is taught is similar to a cult as people are encouraged to accept the NLP principles without question and are not to engage in critical thought. Opposers claim that NLP certifications are administered without careful enough training or testing being carried out. NLP teaching schools have hit back against this criticism and instead insisted that people are free to believe or not believe what they are taught, and that NLP teachers have no means of suppressing free thought. They also insist that people only receive NLO certification after they are ready to, and criticisms in this area stem from the traditional therapy industry worrying about the disruptive potential of NLP.

Chapter 4 - Master Yourself before You Master Others

<u>Self-Mastery First</u>

If you are reading this book it is likely you are seeking to gain a greater sense of influence and control in your life. You probably want to become the kind of person who is able to exert control around anyone and get what they want out of a situation. This is understandable, and this book will provide you with the tools to do exactly that. Before you are ready to exert control over others, however, you must first learn the most important process of all - learning to master yourself.

It is logical to assume that self-mastery is the easiest area of Dark NLP to put into practice. After all, what are we in control of if not ourselves? What you will probably find is that exerting influence over yourself is actually more difficult than exerting influence over others. This is due to the fact that a range of complications come into play in relation to ourselves, such as our own egocentric view of who we are and our inherent resistance to change.

The importance of self-mastery is in line with a wide range of spiritual teachings. All of the major traditions state it is important to gain an insight into the reasons why we behave the way we do and to learn to control our impulses. It is stated that it is this potential for self-control which makes us human and separates us from the animals.

Many people make the mistake of trying to learn advanced ways of getting what they want from others before they first learn to deal with themselves. This is a critical mistake. Our ability to exert control over others is entirely reliant upon our ability to know our own strengths, weaknesses and motivations and how to use these to get what we want out of life. Any attempt to skip past self-mastery will only result in frustration and ineffective outcomes further down the line.

You will now be given the tools and techniques to understand who you are, what you want and how to make sure you get it. You will learn the key ideas behind self-mastery and, more importantly, how to put them to immediate and powerful use. This will allow you to feel focused, energized and influential in absolutely any situation you find yourself in. Most people have only situational confidence, meaning they are able to feel effective provided the environment they are in is familiar. It is far better, however, to feel a deep sense of core confidence that transcends any circumstantial factor. This chapter will provide you with exactly that.

Know Your Outcome

The absolute key to self-mastery from an NLP perspective is always knowing what you want in any given situation. If you are unsure of what you are aiming for then you will never be able to determine the best strategy of how to pursue it. Always have a clear objective in mind and realize that any objective, even if it's imperfect, is better than no objective at all. You can always refine and adjust your goals as you progress towards them and learn more about what you do and do not want.

It is important that you make your intended outcome, your target, as clear and specific as possible. Many people make the mistake of being too vague and setting their goals as something which cannot be measured or assessed. It is vital to avoid that trap and instead ensure your goal is something definitive, which progress towards can be measured, and which has a clear end. Let's explore this through the exploration of an example.

Say, for instance, that you set yourself the objective of gaining a greater amount of choice in your romantic life. A vague way of setting this goal would be to say "I want more choice in my love life." While this goal is able to convey the overall objective, it does not give any indication of how the goal can be fulfilled. A better goal would be to say "I will meet at least five people I can date casually within the next two months." Progress towards the goal can be measured and it has a clear point at which it will have been met. It is also limited by time, which helps to focus a person's efforts and avoid procrastination.

One of the best ways to fix an outcome firmly in mind and make sure it stays as motivational and useful as possible is to envision it in a way which draws upon all of the five senses. You should picture exactly what it would look like to achieve your outcome. What would you see? What would you hear? How would you feel? By making it as real as possible through the process of sensory enrichment, it conditions your mind to see the goal as something real which will occur in the future. As soon as your brain is able to picture the goal as something real it will begin to guide you towards it on a subtle, subconscious level.

Know Your Drives

Knowing your outcome is an essential first step on the path to self-mastery, but it is by no means enough on its own. Without knowing your deepest drives, the very things that motivate you to take massive action in this life, you will be unable to effectively reach your outcome. We will now explore how to uncover your deepest drives and use them to motivate you towards your chosen outcome.

To start with, you should begin to write down anything that comes into your mind when you think of what motivates you. You shouldn't judge or question yourself and just write down anything that you think of. When you can't think of anything new, stop writing. You should have a list of various things in front of you. The exact number will depend upon the personal number of factors that happen to motivate you.

After you have your final list, you should rank the factors in front of you from most to least. Which invokes the greatest feeling of motivation in you when you read it? Which is the second most? Proceed in this way until you have ranked all of the factors. You will now have a clear ranking of your drives in front of you. Write down the top three drives separately, from highest to third highest.

You should now begin the process of linking your top three drives into your chosen outcome. Say for example, you have chosen to lose a certain amount of weight by a certain date. Let's also say that your top three drives happen to be happiness, freedom and health. You can begin to view your goal in terms of how it relates to these drives. You may decide for example, that you will feel a greater sense of confidence and happiness after losing weight, which fulfills your drive for happiness. You think this sense of confidence will help you to feel more liberated and at ease in social situations, which fulfills your need for freedom. Finally, you may wish to focus on the many improvements to your health that will result from losing weight, both in the short and long term. This will help you to stay focused on your goal, even when your motivation inevitably wavers.

<u>Know Your Values</u>

You have now established your intended outcome and linked it on a deep level to the main drives that motivate you in life. This is powerful but to increase your chances of self-mastery even further you should establish your values and similarly link them to your intended outcome.

There is no point in suggesting which values you may wish to consider as it is such a highly personal subject. Just think of the things in life which matter the most to you. Some people find it is helpful to imagine you are running for a position of political office. Which issues do you focus your campaign on? What do you promise the voters? This exercise is powerful to help you have a clear idea of your major values.

Once you have established all of your major values, it is important to rank them in order of the most to least powerful, in the same way that you did with your drives earlier. Once you have established your top three values you should write them down separately.

It is now time to link your values into not only your outcome but also to your drives. By making sure all three of these factors are in alignment, you are able to ensure that you are focused on a deep, subconscious level on achieving your outcome. Think of a major value for you, for example honesty. You can then think of how it ties into your goal and also to your drives. For example, you might think if you are consistently honest you will feel happier, fulfilling your happiness goal. This helps you to ensure all of your motivations are reinforcing each other rather than existing in isolation.

Motivation Is Temporary, Habits Are Not

To achieve your intended outcome you need to have the understanding of your drives and values described above. If you have not taken action on the above section, go back and do it now. It is vital you complete both exercises before proceeding. After doing that, you are ready to establish the two major pillars upon which the rest of your self-mastery rests motivation and habits. Both are essential to move you towards your aims. The key difference between the two is that motivation is quicker to gain but is shorter lasting whereas habits are harder to establish but are longer lasting.

In order to motivate yourself about your outcome, you need to think about all of the ways you will feel good after achieving it. For example, imagine you are seeking a promotion at work. Think not only about the practical changes that will happen in your life after achieving the promotion, but also of how these changes link into deeper aspects such as feelings and values. We will now explore this process through an example.

Let's say, for example, after achieving your promotion you have an increase in salary. You should take a moment to envision this event, and make it real in your mind. What do you feel when picturing it? Perhaps you have a greater sense of security and peace of mind as a result of the extra money. Perhaps you have a greater sense of freedom knowing you are less likely to go into debt in the future. Whatever it is, be sure to find it. Whatever you feel is valid and you just need to ensure that you have your own authentic understanding of the feelings achieving your goal will trigger.

Once you have a clear picture of what achieving your goal will mean for you and the difference it will make in your life, you are able to feel motivated toward attaining it. When your motivation is built on a foundation of understanding the difference your goal will make, you will feel more excited about making it happen, and will therefore increase your chances of doing so.

As stated earlier, motivation is easy to attain, but does not last for a long period of time. For this reason, it is important to build habits that support your outcome. If you do not make a conscious effort to influence your habits you will fall into patterns that do not support your outcome and values in life. In order to form useful habits you must first think of the behaviors you will need to adopt in order to achieve your goal. For example, if your goal is to save more money then you might need to adopt the behaviors of forming a budget and tracking your spending. Each of these behaviors can then be broken down into a smaller series of detailed habits.

For example, to form a budget, you may need to form the habits of recording your spending for a period of time, adding up the total, and dividing the amount into different categories. You may need to form the habit of looking for ways of cutting back on spending, such as finding special offers when out shopping. You may need to form the habit of balancing your budget against your income as part of a wider spending plan.

It is not enough to simply establish habits and motivation in isolation. It is vital that you link them together. You can do this by ensuring you link your motivation to the habits you wish to carry out regularly. This can be supported by the NLP technique of anchoring. For example, you would trigger your state of motivation by envisioning the good feelings triggered by achieving your goal. You would then carry out a repeated physical gesture, such as touching your left wrist while you carry out your routine habit. This subconsciously links the feeling of motivation to the physical gesture. You are then able to trigger the feeling of motivation on command by carrying out the physical trigger of the wrist touch.

It is important to keep track of both your motivation and your habits. One of the best ways to do this is by keeping a journal. At the start of each day you set out what you wish to achieve in terms of attaining motivation and implementing habits. At the end of the day you review your progress in each area and identify factors which led to your success or failure. By doing this you build up a detailed picture over time of what is helping you to succeed and you have the information needed to model your own success.

Energize Your Potential

You now have taken the time to establish a method of summoning motivation on demand and linking this motivation into the habits you have determined are needed to achieve your goals. It is now time to tie all of these separate factors together to ensure you are consistently energized and moving towards your goals. This is done by ensuring you have a full understanding of your potential, your aims and the way of nurturing your potential. All of this will now be explained in a series of easy to carry out, practical steps.

You must first assess the different areas of your life that matter to you. For example, you may be trying to make progress in the areas of money, health and careers. You know need to have a thorough understanding of your potential in each area, in a way which is intended to serve and support you. For example, you may want to firmly envision how you have the potential to earn a lot of money in your lifetime, by thinking of other times you have earned money. You may want to envision what your body will be like after a few months of working out and sticking to a sensible way of eating. You may wish to imagine yourself taking moves towards your dream career, such as by networking online or by gaining new skills.

When you have an understanding of your potential to achieve in each area, you need to think of the particular habits that will serve, support and energize your efforts in each area. For example, if you wish to earn more money, you might want to think about the most useful books to read, the most profitable skills to learn and the most relevant people to network with. When you have a set of clear actions such as this you can take action, confident that your efforts are leading you towards your wider aims.

As well as specific behaviors that are linked to targeted goals, you also should think of habits that will rejuvenate and energize you in general. For example, could you change your sleep schedule to one which provides you with more energy and motivation each day? Can you change your way of eating towards one which is more nutritious and gives you greater levels of drive and focus? Could you change your leisure habits towards those which are able to serve your broader aims?

By finding the areas of life in which you can energize yourself, you provide yourself with a good system of decision making. You can filter any choice through the lens of 'will this energize and move me towards my aims?' This ensures that everything you do is not carried out in isolation, but instead as a step in a wider strategic process aimed to make progress in every area of your life.

Destroy Your Doubts

When you were thinking about the areas of life that mattered to you, and the things you wanted to achieve in them, it is likely that your mind began the process of resistance. It is entirely natural that your mind put forward a range of excuses and doubts as to why you won't succeed. This happens because the human mind is conditioned to seek comfort and activities which do not disturb the status quo. We have the power to overcome this natural inclination but only through exerting conscious will.

There is a process by which you can overcome the doubts in every area of your life. To start with, write down all of the areas that you have previously identified as important, such as wealth, health, relationships and so on. When you have written all of these down, write down all of the doubts that spring to mind with each. For example, with regards to relationships, you may doubt you have the right personality to meet people, or that there is some deficiency with your looks, or that you don't have the right level of income to attract a long-term partner. Don't judge or censor your doubts - just write them all down clearly.

By now you will have a list of doubts associated with each of the main areas of life that you want to progress in. You will now take each of the individual doubts in turn and ask a series of questions about them that is intended to destroy the doubt's power over you. First, ask yourself if anyone in your position has overcome the doubt before. The answer will almost certainly be yes. Then, emphasize to yourself that if others have done it, you can do it too.

Second, you must ask what is the worst that will happen if the doubt is true. For example, if one of your doubts about wealth is losing your job, you might wish to explore what the actual consequences of this would be. You might find you would have a period of lower income but due to your skills and experience you are likely to regain employment quickly. You might further discover you can protect yourself by taking out unemployment insurance. Almost always you will discover that your doubts do not result in nearly as bad an outcome as you feared.

By this point, you have logically demolished the power your doubts previously had over you to make you feel negative emotions. You are now ready to remove them entirely. Begin by writing down for each doubt a series of actions you could take to get rid of it. For example, if one of your doubts is losing your marriage, you could write down a series of actions that would protect against this outcome, such as having regular date nights, being more attentive, giving more compliments and so forth. By doing this you are able to give yourself an easy to follow series of steps which will ensure your doubts are eradicated entirely.

Fight Your Phobias

There is a chance there is some type of phobia in your life that holds you back from feeling as confident as you would like. It is almost impossible to feel as if you are in total control of your life if you know there is one thing that can make you feel irrationally fearful at any time. You will now be given a simple but effective NLP technique which is used to diminish your fears and phobias.

The first important step in this process is to have a clear willingness to face your fears. You have to understand that the process is not easy and may be upsetting at times. After you have firmly intended to see the process through, you must begin by envisioning the thing that you fear. Say, for example, that the object of your fears is tall places. You should close your eyes and picture yourself somewhere high up. See it clearly and sharply and be fully aware of what it makes you feel.

Once you have a clear mental image of the thing you fear, begin by blurring the picture in your mind. Imagine the quality of the picture has been lowered, as if it was taken on an older camera. Notice how your level of fear towards the phobia has lessened. Continue to distort the picture and shrink it down. Picture it being shrunk and losing all clarity until it is an unidentifiable blur. Notice how your fear towards the trigger has diminished entirely?

After you have consistently gotten into the habit of reducing your fear through this process, you should automatically carry it out whenever the trigger for your phobia arises. You will notice that your level of fear steadily diminishes, until you no longer have to repeat the process, because your fear towards the situation has diminished entirely.

You now know the process by which NLP is used to eradicate phobias. Next we will explore some of the most common phobias that NLP is used to treat. For each phobia that is identified, the role of NLP in positively changing a person's life will be highlighted. This is intended to inspire people suffering from the various phobias to take action to eradicate them once and for all.

Heights is one of the most common phobias that people have, as it is one of the few that we have as the result of instinct, rather than learned fear. People often try and use NLP to confront their fear of heights. A range of techniques exist that enable people to first reframe the way they feel about heights, and then remove the ability of heights to impact their emotions for good.

First, an NLP practitioner will help people to overcome any shame or judgment someone has about their fear of heights. People often tell themselves they are weak or bad for fearing heights. A powerful reframe to take in this situation is to instead see a fear of heights as something praiseworthy. Being aware of our fear of heights simply means we have a good sense of danger perception. It is nothing to be ashamed of. Just because we accept it, however, it does not mean we grant it power to influence our lives.

An NLP technique which is often used to remove the emotional power of phobias such as heights involves asking the individual to envision being in a high place in their mind. They then disassociate from the image by seeing themselves in the third person rather than seeing things through a first person point of view. By doing this, they will see that their fear lessens, as they are able to effectively remove themselves from being directly involved with the feared situation.

In doing this, the individual is made to realize that they are able to control how connected they feel with a situation, and therefore how much power it has over their emotions. By repeatedly making a feared situation less personal and viewed in the third person, a person becomes able to carry out this process when faced with the fear for real. They become so conditioned to detach from the situation that they are able to do so in real life.

Chapter 5 - Take Control of Others

Now that you have a sufficient understanding of yourself through the principles of NLP to understand and leverage your outcomes, drives and values, you will be shown how to extend this self-mastery over others. You will learn the techniques which allow you to gain a total understanding of what makes a person act the way they do and how to influence them through both your actions and your words. You should use these techniques with caution in real life as their power cannot be overstated.

<u>Hacking Anyone's Secret Blueprint</u>

The first step to gaining a level of influence over someone is to figure out their unique 'secret blueprint' that makes them who they are. There are several aspects of a person you need to understand in order to gain potential control over them. These are their fears, their hopes, their doubts, the things they like about themselves and the things they dislike about themselves. You will now be shown how to figure out all of these aspects of a person's blueprint and how to take action based on this information to increase the level of influence over someone you have.

In order to understand someone's fears, there are two main methods you can use. These can be used either in isolation or in conjunction. The first method is the passive method and involves simply paying close attention to what a person talks about in order to determine the things that worry them. Different people are more or less obvious in the way they reveal this aspect of themselves. Some people talk about things and clearly state they are worried by them, while others are not explicit about this and instead hint at it through their tone of voice and general demeanor when discussing certain issues.

In addition to passively listening to someone to determine the aspects of life they are fearful about, it is possible to actively explore the issue by mentioning certain things. For example, you may wish to casually lead the conversation towards the topic of health. Depending on how the person responds in terms of their willingness to talk, their tone of voice and their physical comfort levels, you will be able to gauge how much of a worry health is to that person. You can use this approach to gauge a person's fear towards any particular issue. However, you should only use this method once or twice per conversation in order to ensure the person does not detect your attempts.

Uncovering a person's hopes is often easier than determining their fears. This is because people often give away what they aspire to in life by disclosing their aims for the future. Even seemingly trivial aspects of a person, such as the choice of purchases they make, can indicate the way they see themselves and what they aspire to be seen as by others.

A great way of encouraging someone to open up about their hopes is by talking about your own hopes. This often prompts the other person to become candid about what they are personally aiming towards in life. A manipulative, Dark NLP spin on this method is to disclose insincere hopes that are specifically intended to increase your target's comfort level towards a certain topic. For example, you may say you have some money worries, even though you do not. This is manipulatively chosen to make your target feel as if the issue of money worries is acceptable to talk about. By taking the lead you are granting them permission to open up. It is important to keep track of the story you have told any given person, however, in order to ensure you don't contradict yourself.

To figure out a person's doubts is often just a case of seeing the areas of life in which they behave confidently, and those in which they behave more cautiously. When someone behaves with ease and a feeling of self-belief it is a sign that that person feels competent and effective in that area of their life. Conversely, when someone behaves with more doubt and hesitancy, it is a sign that you have uncovered one of their weak points. It is important to remember this information as it can be used to influence the person in a technique that will be explained shortly.

Perhaps the most obvious aspect to figure out about someone is the things they like and dislike about themselves. There are very few people who are able to act in a way which effectively conceals the aspects of their personality and appearance that they are sure about, and those which they are not. The way in which a person behaves in different situations, their comfort around strangers and even the clothes they wear are all powerful indicators about how someone feels about themselves.

One simple but effective way of gauging someone's overall level of self-esteem in any given area is to pay them a targeted compliment. For example, if you want to figure out how someone feels about their own looks, you should say they look good one day. If they are comfortable with how they look, they will accept the compliment with ease and warmth. If they are not happy with how they look then they will become uncomfortable and possibly attempt to reject the compliment or change the subject.

When you know someone's hopes and fears you can use them to influence the choices the person makes. For example, you may wish for someone to act in a certain way towards someone else within your workplace. To do this, you should contrast two options for the person - the one you want, and the opposite course of action. You should link your description to the action you want to the person's deepest hopes and use language related to the person's fears to the course of action you wish to avoid. This is a subtle NLP technique known as embedded language which plays upon a person's own personal blueprint to steer a course of action.

You can also use the things that people like and dislike about themselves to manipulate them. For example, you can lower or raise a person's self-esteem to suit your own purposes. To raise a person's self-esteem, you can pay them a compliment which draws upon the aspirational view they have of themselves. By agreeing with this ideal view you are building a sense of rapport between you. This technique is useful if you wish to influence them to do something which requires confidence.

You can also lower a person's self-esteem as needed by subtly insulting them in a way which plays upon their fears and dislikes about themselves. It is important to do this in a way which ensures that the insult is masked and embedded rather than being obvious. For example, if the person has insecurities related to how they come across around new people, you could choose to exclude them from speaking in a meeting, and afterwards comment to them how you thought it didn't play to their strengths. By doing this you establish yourself as someone who has authority over a person. By being able to lower their self esteem you send a strong signal to their subconscious that the person is under your control and of a lower standing than you psychologically.

How to Read Someone's Eyes

It has often been said that a person's eyes are the windows to their soul. If that is the case then this section of the book will show you how to read a person's eye movements to determine their deepest secrets, such as whether they are lying or being truthful in any given situation.

To begin reading a person's eye movements, it is first important to ask a series of questions and make a mental note of the person's direction of eye movement as they answer. Start by asking the person something factual that they will answer truthfully, such as their date of birth. Where do they look? Is it to the left, the right? Up, or down? The direction of the person's eye movements as they answer is indicative of the eye movement that they make when they are telling the truth.

Next, ask the person something that requires them to use their imagination. For example, ask them how they would spend their winnings if they were to win the lottery. The person's eyes will move to a specific direction as they are using their imagination, often up and slightly off to the side. This is the direction that indicates the person is using imagination to construct what they are saying. If you ask the person a question in the future, and their eyes move in this way, then it means that they are inventing the answer they are telling you.

Finally, you should ask a question that is intended to provoke a lie from the person. For example, if you know they are insecure about their salary, ask them if they make a figure that is slightly higher than they actually make. The chances are they will agree with you as they do not want to reveal the lower amount they are insecure about. The movement their eyes make, and their tone of voice, can be used to detect when they are lying about something in the future.

You now have the range of eye movements that a person makes that indicate whether they are being truthful, inventing an answer or lying about an answer. You can always use this to determine whether that person is being sincere with you and also to find out their insecurities by seeing what they lie about.

Linguistic Mind Control

A person's choice of language is a powerful indication of what drives them and the way they see the world. For example, people will often show their agreement by saying either "I see what you mean," "I know what you mean," "I hear you," or "'that feels right." Their choice of language in this area shows whether their primary way of perceiving the world is through their sight, their ears their touch or their logic. When you know their primary system of perception you can explain things you want them to agree with in language drawing upon their primary system, and explain ideas you wish them to disagree with in language that goes against their system.

People will also disclose words that have a special level of meaning or significance for them. For example, you might notice that a person always uses the word 'brilliant' to explain someone they deeply admire. They only use the word when they are in a state of heightened emotion. This is a sign that the word has a strong level of significance to them. You can use this to your advantage by deploying the word in your own statements when you wish to trigger a deep level of agreement with what you say. You should use this sparingly however, as overusing it will make your intentions obvious and come across as unnatural.

A person's choice of words also often changes with their internal state and over time you will learn to read which words indicate which internal state. This is useful as you can modify your own behavior and choice of words to ensure it is compatible with their internal view of the world. This creates a sense of rapport between the two of you, which allows you to exert greater levels of undetected influence over the person's mind. You will now be shown in detail how to gain physical rapport with someone and then begin to lead the pace of the interaction.

Mirror Someone to Enslave Their Mind

The first step to being able to take control of someone's physicality as well as his or her inner state is to become a keen observer of body language. You need to be able to take constant notice of the people you interact with and the way they hold themselves, the way they move, their expressions, the way their position their feet and the way they position their hands. It is essential to learn to notice even the smallest detail that people exhibit. This is because learning to mimic a person's body language effectively is one of the quickest ways to create a deep sense of rapport with them.

After you have noticed a person's particular body language, you should learn to become adept at mirroring it. This Dark NLP technique gives you the ability to create a deep, artificial sense of rapport and commonality with someone without them being aware it is down to your influence. To begin with, you should copy one aspect of a person's body language only, such as the way they position their arms. You should then start to mirror more and more of them, one aspect at a time, until you are holding yourself in exactly the same way that they are.

Once you have totally mirrored someone's body language in the way that is described above you should begin to subtly copy any changes they make. For example, if the person you are mirroring shifts the position of their left arm, you should move yours in a similar way. This will ensure that the sense of rapport they are feeling is maintained.

There are several ways that you can check if you have achieved the desired level of rapport with your target. The main way is through physical leading, which will be described in detail in this chapter's next section. Some of the things you may notice after you have effectively mirrored someone's body language is that they find it far easier to open up to you. They may become warmer in their emotional tone and more free in their disclosing of information. They may also more readily agree with opinions you express. This is because they feel a deep, subconscious level of agreement with you and this manifests in their thoughts as well as their words.

Taking Control through Pacing and Leading

One of the most effective ways of checking your mirroring has worked well and created the sense of connection you intended it to is by attempting to take control of the interaction physically. How is this done? The first stage of the process is to mirror someone for a period of time, including subtly copying any changes to their body language they make. After doing this for a while, attempt to be the first one to take the lead in making a small change to your own body language. For example, you can move the position of your right hand. Ideally, the person you have been mirroring will copy your body language.

When someone copies the changes to your body language, it shows that they are in a deep feeling of rapport with you and are willing to be led by you on a subconscious level. In this state, they are highly influential and this is a prime time to get them to agree with you or to carry out any other manipulations you desire. If, however, when you attempt to lead the interaction, they do not copy you, all is not lost. Just mirror them for a while longer and eventually attempt to lead the interaction once more. Eventually, you will have created enough subconscious rapport for them to follow your lead.

The key to effectively leading someone in this way is to begin by making small leads and then gradually work your way up to making bigger changes to your body language. For example, begin by making a small change to the position of your hand, then move an entire arm, and then do some more bold movement, such as moving both arms at once. The greater the level of mirroring your target shows, the greater the amount of rapport you have built with them, and therefore you can influence them to a corresponding extent.

Chapter 6 - Take Control of the Past, Present and Future

One of the most powerful aspects of NLP is the ability to take control of all three personal dimensions of time - your past, present and future. Many of the self help or personal development techniques available in the world today make a halfhearted attempt to focus on one aspect only, such as by promoting a better today, or a more hopeful tomorrow. Dark NLP does not rely on such a limited outlook. Because its principles are grounded in reliable scientific evidence, it is as effective in one time as in any other.

In this chapter, you will first be taught how to see the world according to the concepts of Dark NLP. Some of the classic NLP concepts are updated and refined in light of the latest dark psychology knowledge discoveries. These will be explained not only as ideas but also shown to be actionable and directly useful in multiple areas of your life.

The purpose of this chapter is to train you to see the world through the lens of Dark NLP. This is by no means the 'true' view of the world - as any single outlook is bound to be subjective - but is a very useful view to take should you choose to pursue it. You will first be taught how to see things as exploitable opportunities and to assess the balance of power in any given situation.

You will then be encouraged to use Dark NLP to make the most of your past, enhance your present reality and build the future that you really desire. Specific techniques are given such as reframes of the past, mantras for the present and powerful tools to build your ideal future.

Seeing the World According to Dark NLP

This section is one of the most important in the entire book as it provides you with a way of seeing the world that will enable you to become effective and take control of your circumstances, rather than vice versa. You will now be given a series of concepts and viewpoints that reflect the core principles of NLP filtered through the lens of dark psychology to result in Dark NLP's primary rules of understanding.

The first key understanding you must reach is it doesn't so much matter what you do or say - what matters is the result you are able to attain. If this sounds very results oriented and tactical, it's because it is. This way of viewing the world presents either a threat or an opportunity to most people. Some people, upon hearing that they should focus only on the result, protest that it is important to do things in the right way. Other people instantly feel comfortable with the idea of pursuing an outcome relentlessly and getting there by any means necessary. No matter your initial reaction, it is important you eventually come to realize the importance of achieving an intended result over any other consideration.

So what are some of the ways in which you can put the idea of focusing only on results into practice? Let's first consider the professional world. Imagine you are a manager who is trying to motivate an employee. What would be the

Dark NLP view of the situation? That the only thing that matters is your ability to get through to the employee and increase their level of motivation. This may conflict with other ideas about management, such as those which state that employees should be spoken to in a certain way, or that managers should always adopt a particular tone. Dark NLP teaches that the manager should do or say whatever it takes to achieve the desired outcome. The result is the only thing that matters.

The second core mental attitude required for Dark NLP is to understand that absolutely everything is completely subjective, and even if people use the same words they may have entirely different meanings associated with the words in their mind. So what does this mean practically? It is important to never assume that you know what someone means when they use a certain word unless you have evidence of their specific meaning. It also requires you to understand that two people can be sharing in the same event but assign a totally different meaning to it in their mind. For example, a couple may be getting married. For one person, they are participating in an important religious event. For the other, they may be doing no more than participating in a socially mandated tradition. Always understand that people assign their own meanings to events.

So what are some of the implications of the above Dark NLP teaching? Firstly, it means that effective users of Dark NLP are able to influence the way in which people perceive what is happening to them. Let's take an example from within the world of management. Let's say a manager needed their workers to work some extra hours to get an important project wrapped up. In the workers' minds, at least initially, they may feel that they are being exploited. If the manager is a skilled user of Dark NLP, however, they will be able to tie the extra work into the workers' values and give it a better meaning, such as making a sacrifice for the greater good. Once you realize nothing has any absolute, objective meaning, you are free to manipulate the subjective meaning of things to your own advantage.

Dark NLP also emphasizes the fact the language people use is not an absolute representation of what they are thinking or feeling. We have touched on this already but will now expand on it further. For example, two people may use the word 'fine' to describe how they are feeling. Assuming they mean the same thing in both cases would be a huge mistake. Over the years of their life, both people would have built up a series of reference experiences, and meanings for them, which they have come to associate with the word 'fine.' For any given word a person uses, they have an entire history supporting exactly what they mean by it. Failing to take into account this highly subjective use of language means you will never be able to understand people on a deeply personal level.

So what are some of the practical uses of this subjective understanding of language? It requires you to become attuned to not only the words that people say but also the emotional tone with which they say them. You need to look past the surface, obvious meaning of the word and figure out the precise meaning it has for the individual that is using it. Once you have figured out the precise meaning of words for the people that are using them you are in a position to mirror the words back and influence them on a deep, subconscious level.

Dark NLP teaches you to understand that there is no true difference between a person's physical being and their mind - indeed they are part of a single system that works in harmony. After all, the body cannot move without commands from the mind, and the mind is useless without a body to control. Once you understand that the body and mind are part of the same system, rather than existing in isolation, you further reach the understanding that the state of one impacts upon the state of the other. For example, when your body is tired out, perhaps from physical exertion, there is less energy available for your mind and you process things slower. Similarly, if you deprive your mind of sleep and feel tired as a result, your bodily movements will be slower. This teaches you to treat both your body and your mind well as one reinforces the other.

In order to use Dark NLP effectively, you should always use it with a view to increasing the amount of choice you have at any given time. For example, one of the core teachings of NLP that has been updated and used in Dark NLP, states that the more choices that are available to a person, the more likely they are to be able to achieve their intended outcome. So how does a person use the concepts of Dark NLP to increase the level of choice they experience? Firstly, they can use the tips in this book to create a deep sense of rapport with almost everyone they meet. By doing this, you ensure that your network is as wide as possible and you have a connection for any need you may encounter.

One of the key end products of Dark NLP is the requirement for the person using it to be as flexible and adaptable as possible to the situation that they find themselves in. Dark NLP teaches that any seemingly permanent situation is in fact temporary and liable to change, so you should never become reliant upon any particular set of circumstances. Instead, you should learn to be as adaptable as possible because the conditions you find yourself in are bound to change.

With the above teaching in mind, there are a range of ways you can focus on ensuring you are as adaptable and resolute as possible. Firstly, it is important that you experience life in a range of different conditions. For example, it is important to go through times of more and less money. It is only when you have experienced times of less that you can appreciate they are not the end of the world. As soon as you become comfortable with the state of affairs you previously feared it loses its power to intimidate you.

Dark NLP teaches that you should always evaluate your behavior, or the behavior of others, in terms of the results it generates in the context in which it takes place. That is to say, no behavior can be judged as inherently good or bad. What works in one situation might be ineffectual in another, and what fails in one context might be the right move in another situation. It may be hard to let go of preconceptions of what is right and wrong but it is needed in order to move towards a frame of judging things only by their outcome.

In order to make a mental switch from thinking in terms of doing the right or wrong thing, begin to always ask yourself the question "What is the intended outcome if I take this course of action? What is the likely outcome? Is there a better course of action I could take instead?" By asking these questions, you rapidly gain the ability to always think in terms of outcome and the best way to get there, rather than judging your actions by some other criteria.

Perhaps the most key insight into people taught by NLP, and later adapted for Dark NLP, is the fact that a person's behavior is the most important source of information we can access about them. People are capable of saying almost anything about themselves in order to come across in a certain way. The way they behave, on the other hand, is far harder to fake over a prolonged period of time, and is therefore far more indicative of what a person's character is truly like. It is always worth observing someone's behavior and assessing it in terms of how well it matches with the way they have portrayed their self verbally. By doing this, you will soon see the disparity between a person's portrayal and actuality.

This concept of behavior within Dark NLP is understood on a deeper level when a clear distinction is drawn between it and the concept of self. It is important to realize that NLP emphasizes that a person's self is not defined by their behavior. This is evidenced by the fact that inherently good people are capable of behaving badly, and people who are inherently bad can behave well from time to time. In order to understand someone through the lens of NLP it is worth seeing them as behaving in a certain way, rather than being a certain way. This is further understood through dark psychology by seeing people as having a very fluid sense of self - they behave and adapt according to their best understanding of what any given situation requires.

One of the implications of the distinction between self and behavior in Dark NLP is that we should aim to influence a person's behavior rather than their self. Since someone's self is a fluid concept that is ultimately unknowable, the best that we can hope for is to influence a person's behavior. Since this would be the ultimate intended outcome of altering their self, it is more efficient to influence their behavior initially.

Dark NLP teaches you to never judge yourself, especially through the lens of conventional morality, and to understand that you have never truly failed; you have only received feedback that you need to try a different course of action. The only true failure is to stop trying as it is stated that as long as someone is willing to try for, they always have another chance of reaching their aim. Someone may need to try many different strategies in life until they find one that is right for their context. We should emotionally detach from our actions and realize they do not reflect upon who we are, rather they only show what we thought was the most effective approach to take at the time.

<u>Master Your Past</u>

The core NLP understandings covered above will now be filtered down into a series of actionable steps you can take to gain control over the three personal dimensions of time, starting with your past.

In order to get the most out of this exercise, you need to be willing to be truly honest with yourself. You need to be willing to face all of the choices you have made in life and analyze them in terms of the results they generated and the lessons you can learn from them. This is not as painful as you imagine, as you will not be doing this in an emotional way. You will not be judging yourself. Instead, you will be dispassionately looking back over your life and identifying a list of choices you made and the results they generated.

In order to do this, think back to a major decision you made in your life. It could be something external, such as the choice of university to study at, or something internal, such as the choice to no longer be unhappy. Whatever it was, you should jot down a summarized title for the choice, such as 'being happy' or 'choosing university'. It is important that you physically write this down, as the act of doing so has been shown to help you process information on a deeper level.

After you have written down the name of the decision, write down the series of choices that you had at the time. This should include the actual decision that you made, and the range of alternative choices that you chose not to use. You should write down as many alternatives as you can, but try to think back to your actual thought process at the time, rather than imagining how you felt.

You should now have the range of choices for the decision that you made. It is now time to remember the thought process you went through when making your choice. Did you try to think through the pros and cons of each option rationally? Did you go with a gut feeling? Whatever your decision making process was, write it down to the best of your ability.

Now it is time to write down the outcome of your decision. Did it go as intended? If so, what do you attribute as the critical success factors? If the decision you made did not result in your intended outcome, why was this? What could you have done differently to ensure a different outcome? Try to summarize the key lessons of every outcome - positive or negative.

By this point, you should have condensed your thought process behind each major decision, and concisely summarized the main takeaway learning points. If you do this for other major choices in your life, you will soon see patterns emerge. You may notice that a particular method of decision making seems to result in your intended outcome being achieved. If this is the case, take some time to write down and analyze why this method of decision making achieves the results it does. Then, write down some ways which will help you to make sure you use this particular decision making process in the future.

You will often find that is the most painful parts of your past, the ones you try to keep hidden, that end up offering the most profound levels of insight. This can cause pain, immense pain even, in the short term but benefits you over the longer term. This is because the most painful parts of our past are the ones which retain the ability to impact upon our emotional state, even into the present time. By learning to take control of our past's most painful points and use them as powerful lessons to make us wiser in the future, we remove the emotional trauma of our past and instead channel it into a positive outcome in the present.

You now have a method to learn lessons from your past. When you are able to wrap your head around this frame and take action on it, you will soon see that there is no need to regret anything that has happened in your past, as everything is a valuable learning experience.

Perfect Your Present

Dark NLP is something that not only gives you a profound understanding of your past, and gives you a way to directly shape your future, but also allows you to live fully in the present moment. Dark NLP aims to give tools to immediately increase your levels of satisfaction, as well as aiming to increase these in the future. One way in which Dark NLP is able to satisfy your present is by giving you permission to unlock your truest, deepest desires, the ones you really have, not the ones you feel socially pressured into proclaiming.

There is a method by which you can explore your deepest desires through a series of simple but powerful questions. First, you should ask yourself how you would spend a free day if no one else were around to see it. Second, you should think about how you would spend a lottery win if no one knew what you would buy. Finally, you should ask yourself which crime you would commit if you were guaranteed to get away with it and no one would ever find out.

By giving honest answers to the above questions, you will see what your real desires are. The power of the questions is it requires you to think in a way that takes the judgment of other people out of the equation. By doing this you allow yourself to express what it is you truly want. The answers you give may surprise you or you may feel inherently at ease with them. Either way, make note of what it is you truly desire, as you are about to apply it in a way which enhances your present.

Once you have figured out your true desire, think about it on a deeper level. For example, think of a situation in which you had uncovered your deepest desire was to have more money. If this was the case, you should think about what the money represents for you. Perhaps it would represent a greater sense of freedom. If that was the case, you should combine both the desire itself and its deeper representation into a mantra. An example using this situation would be "I will acquire money and I will experience freedom." You can then incorporate repetitions of these mantras into your daily routines. It is important to try to feel the emotions while saying the mantras. By reciting these regularly, you train your brain to focus on attracting your deepest desires.

You can also use your increased emotional perception and understanding that comes with Dark NLP practice to figure out which activities in your life give you the best results at different times. For example, it is likely that you use a series of different methods to relax. Perhaps sometimes you go for a walk, other times you mediate. By using NLP to rationally and non judgmentally analyze your own behavior, you will be able to determine when certain actions give you results, and when they prove to be ineffective.

It is also important to engage in activities in the present that are able to energy and support you. For example, it is essential to figure out the physical triggers which stimulate your peak states. Some people for example respond well to building a routine in which they listen to a song that pumps them up while thinking of their past achievements. They may also adopt a particular physical pose while doing this. Such routines are ways of shortcutting the normal process and achieving a peak state of power and creativity in a short amount of time.

Create Your Future

Dark NLP provides you with techniques that effectively allow you to hack into your own brain and brainwash yourself into moving towards your aims on autopilot. To do this, you first need to tap into the most primal system of reward that exists within you. You are going to use a visceral feeling of achievement to drive your inner being towards your goals. First, you need to picture a time when you have achieved something you set out to do. Think of the raw feeling that accompanied your triumph, perhaps it was the feeling of exhilaration and sheer happiness. It is important that you recall this state as thoroughly as you can and really try to picture it in as much detail that you almost feel it is happening now. It is important that you eventually reach the stage where you are able to summon this feeling on demand.

You are now going to picture the achievement of three goals in your mind that you want to happen within the next year. For example, you might see yourself getting your driving license, kissing the person you desire and receiving a certificate of education. You are now going to brainwash yourself into linking these concepts to your deepest sense of triumph, and making your brain feel as if it has already experienced your intended outcomes.

To do this, you need to picture one of your intended outcomes as clearly as you can. Picture it in as much detail as you are capable of, and hold this image firmly in your mind's focus. Now, make the picture even brighter and more vivid in your mind's eye. While you do this mental resizing, summon the feeling of triumph that you practiced in the last exercise. Link it deeply in your mind to the picture of your intended outcome. Link them to one another until you are unable to picture your outcome in your mind without triggering the sense of triumph. Repeat this exercise with the two other short-term goals you have set yourself.

By doing this, you trick your subconscious into associating a future event with a feeling you have already had. You brain is unable to separate the two, so your mind accepts the intended outcome as if it has already happened. As a result of this, your brain is primed for it to occur, and will actively seek out to make it happen. This is to ease the cognitive dissonance that occurs as a resulting of feeling as if something is in the past, while in fact it has yet to occur.

You can also picture ahead and envision what your life will look like in the future. A common time period for this exercise is five or ten years. When doing this, you should imagine your home environment for that future period. What will it look like? What view will you have? What will the room be like? You should try to make the picture as rich in terms of sensory data as possible. Imagine the sights you will see, the smell of the room, the feel of the carpet and the sounds of the environment. By making the idea as rich as possible you make it more realistic to your own brain.

By picturing this image and recalling its rich sensory data as often as possible, you train your mind to accept it as something that is possible and within your reach. It also serves as a powerful motivation. Whenever you are feeling some resistance to taking action and completing a particular task, you will be able to recall the rich sensory image of your desired future home. By doing this, you will realize that it is essential to take action in order to make the vision a reality. This allows you to summon motivation on demand and always make any task, no matter how trivial, part of a meaningful whole.

Chapter 7 - Take What You Want Without Apology

The Right Frame

Up until this point in the book, the focus has been on understanding the foundations of Dark NLP and understanding how it is applied to gain control of yourself and of others. You will now move from a people-based frame to an outcome-based frame. Instead of thinking of Dark NLP in terms of how it allows you to influence people, including yourself, you will learn to think of it in terms of how it allows you to get what you want.

You can think of the previous sections of this book as the toolkit which you need in order to carry out the tasks of this chapter. Your understanding of yourself, others and your desires in life will now combine into a series of practical steps that allows you to ruthlessly seize whatever it is you want out of life. Techniques will be provided that will make success second nature to you and tips will be given on how to ensure you don't sell yourself short in life and take everything from it you can.

The first step in being able to get what you want out of life is having the right frame. You will recall that one of the core concepts in Dark NLP is that there is no objective picture of reality, only a subjective interpretation of it. As a result of this, the way in which you frame any given situation has a big impact upon how effective you are within it. The right frame to have when seeking out your desires in life is "I deserve to get what I want out of life."

The above frame may sound simple, but it can be hard to achieve, for a variety of reasons. Some people struggle with the sense of entitlement that is required to make the most of this frame. You need to feel as if you truly deserve whatever good happens to you in life. Other people have trouble accepting the fact that the frame makes the distinction between want and need, and you should aim to get everything you want, not only the basic needs. It is difficult for some people to accept that they deserve a life of luxury. They therefore limit themselves and are their own obstacle in getting the most out of life.

In order to make the most of life, you need to understand that there is no scarcity of opportunities and resources. As much as people like to complain in our modern world, we live in a time of unparalleled possibility. Anyone is able to access the sum total of the world's information via the internet, from anywhere using their smartphone. Any skill, any subject, any idea - everything can be explored instantaneously.

Because of this absolute abundance of opportunity, you should realize that by you succeeding and getting what you want out of life does not mean there is less for other people to get. Indeed, by becoming successful you are actually putting yourself in a position to give more back to the world. Once you are able to see that you getting what you want doesn't deprive anyone else, you will be able to approach the goal with a greater sense of purpose, free from any doubt or guilt.

Morning Routines

One of the foundations of getting what you want out of life is to build a series of routines and habits which enable you to achieve consistently. This chapter will now focus on providing you with a process that constructs morning and evening routines that help you to stay focused on your path, focused on your success, and refining your approach as you go. The routines will be personal for you and exist specifically to serve your unique needs and situation.

The essential purpose of a morning routine is to put yourself into a state of focus, flow and peak performance. By carrying out a series of actions in a consistent order, day after day, you make your transition from sleep to achievement as smooth and predictable as possible. By reducing any variation you eliminate the potential for distractions or surprises to draw you away from your productivity. So what exactly does a morning routine consist of?

The first step for many people when constructing their morning routine is to take a refreshing shower. By refreshing the body, the mind is refreshed also. This ties in with the earlier core Dark NLP principle that the mind and body exist as one connected system, rather than in isolation. When showering, it is suggested that the person takes the time to either meditate, or repeat success mantras in their mind. The way in which such mantras can be formed has been detailed earlier in the book. You should also use products that enliven and awaken the senses, such as those containing menthol or invigorating natural ingredients.

The next stage of the morning routine for many people is preparing some kind of food or beverage that is in line with their specific nutritional goals. Some of the most common options are to prepare either a specialized type of coffee, known as the bulletproof coffee, or to make a fresh smoothie containing a range of health boosting ingredients. Some followers of peak performance diets, such as the slow carb diet, take this opportunity to prepare a protein rich breakfast. Whichever approach you take to this step of the routine should be aligned with your wider health aims and ideas.

Next, you should enjoy the beverage or food you produced while going over your goals for the day. Everyone has a different system for representing what they intend to do over the course of the day. Some people prefer handwritten to do lists, others prefer apps and some people write out tasks on a whiteboard - the specific technique does not matter. What does matter is having a clear, written series of outcomes for the day ahead, and taking the time to review these and set them in your mind.

Some people prefer the next stage of their morning routine to delve into the most important or challenging task on their to-do list for the day. Others prefer to take some time out before getting going on the day to indulge in a nurturing activity, such as reading something enlightening or meditating. Some people find that taking the time for this step of the morning routine allows them to carry out their tasks for the day in a more focused and productive way.

<u>Evening Routines</u>

Think of the morning and evening routines as two complementary pieces of the same puzzle. They are two boundaries of the day and by establishing them, you train your mind to think in terms of achieving a series of aims between the two bookmarks of the routines. So what exactly does an evening routine consist of, and what are its main objectives?

A successful evening routine has two main purposes - to relax the body and mind and prepare it for rest, and to reflect upon what has taken place during the day in terms of the outcomes attained. The order of the routine varies from person to person, and by experimenting with different routines, you will eventually find out what works for you. However, most routines consist of a mixture of the following processes.

Many people think the evening is a great time to meditate. Typically, by the end of the day, we will have accumulated a lot of baggage and stress. Our interactions with others over the course of the day will play out in our minds, and this can even sometimes stop us from sleeping. In order to empty our minds of our woes, meditation can be effective. It does not require a lot of time, and anyone can teach themselves how to perform it effectively. To meditate for relaxation and calm in the evening, try the following steps.

Firstly, get in a comfortable position, either sitting up or lying down. Close your eyes and take a series of deep breaths. Make sure that your focus is on the physical sensations present in your body. Begin by tensing your toes, and holding them tight for several seconds. Then, allow your toes to relax, and notice the feeling of calm that floods into them. Sequentially work your way up your body, tensing each body part, and then relaxing it. Your awareness should be totally on your body, and away from your thoughts.

By the time you have worked your way up to your eyelids you should be feeling totally relaxed. It is not time to stop. Instead, picture the feeling of relaxation you experience as a small ball of white light. Where is the light located on your body? Is it glowing? Is it moving? Make the picture as real as you can in your mind. Once you can picture the ball of light clearly, allow it to grow and expand. Picture it growing larger and larger, until it has surrounded your body. Allow your body to spend some time soaking in this relaxing white light, until a sense of deep relaxation permeates your whole being. Slowly, open your eyes.

Once you are in a state of total relaxation, you can begin to analyze the day you have just experienced. You may wish to look back upon your written list of goals you reviewed at the start of the day. Which of them were you able to achieve? Which of them did you not achieve? What enabled you to achieve the goals you did, and what prevented you from meeting the ones you did not? By getting into the habit of analyzing your goals as part of your evening routine, you will begin to be able to identify the factors consistently linked with your triumphs and failures.

You may also wish to incorporate into your evening routine a process of visualizing the following day. This should involve having a clear image in your mind of how you want your tomorrow to pan out and the things you will achieve. By taking the time to visualize this, you prime your mind to make it happen, and you will be subtly influenced into taking actions that move you closer towards your intended outcome.

Some people also find the end of their evening routine a great time to keep an in depth journal. Unlike a regular journal, there is some specific areas of focus that make a Dark NLP journal unique. Rather than simply recording what has happened to you in the course of the day, you should focus on recording your internal thought processes at the time. You should also spend time pondering why you have arrived at the subjective understanding of the day, for example why has another meaning not seemed a better fit to you? By doing this, you will gain a greater understanding of your own thought processes and the way in which your mind operates. You can use this information to model your own peak states and enter into them more consistently.

Celebrate Success

One of the most important psychological concepts informing the Dark NLP concept is that of operant conditioning. This basically states that a person will be more likely to carry out a behavior if they experience a positive reward for doing so. It is up to you to put this understanding into action and celebrate your successes. By doing this, you condition your mind to seek out success as it links positive feelings with the attainment of goals. So how exactly should you take action on this idea?

The first step to take is to grant yourself permission to feel fully happy and without any shame or doubt when you achieve your aims. You should literally tell yourself positive, supportive statements of praise that reinforce to your subconscious that you are someone who is able to achieve, and who feels good when they do so. By doing this, you give your mind permission and space to link success to happiness.

It can be good to provide yourself with a tangible reward when you achieve an aim. For example, buy yourself a luxury item that is proportionate to the scale of the success achieved. By doing this, you teach your mind to link acquisition of desired things with the attainment of success. The material reward of success is often not experienced until further down the line. The human brain, however, has evolved to focus on short-term reward as a method of survival. You can turn this to your advantage by providing an immediate material reward to yourself whenever you succeed.

The Power of Peer Groups

One of the most commonly overlooked factors when trying to get what you want out of life is the role that the people around you play. Dark NLP gives you the tools you need to build rapport with people and add them into your peer group at will. Given that you have this ability, you owe it to yourself to build the peer group that will help you to get what you want out of life, and live the lifestyle of your deepest desires. So how exactly do you determine which peer group will be best suited to achieving your aims, and how do you bring them into your life?

Psychological research shows that the people we are closest to influence us in a number of ways. For example, if our closest friends are overweight, it is likely that we ourselves will become overweight. There have been a number of explanations for this. Some people believe that our peer group dictates to us what is normal and therefore acceptable. Others believe that we pick up habits and choices from our peer group at a deep, subconscious level. Whatever the explanation, one thing is certain - the choice of people we have around is a significant factor in the lifestyle we experience.

This book has given you the tools to determine exactly what it is you desire from this world, free from the shackles of others' judgment. If you take a minute to picture these desires, you can also imagine the type of people who would help you get to where you want to be. For example, if your goal is to experience an abundance of success within the world of romantic encounters, it might be useful for you to have a peer group of other adventurous, single friends. Similarly, if your goal revolved around achieving academic excellence, would it not benefit you to have a social circle consisting of academic high achievers? No matter what your goal, there is a peer group that is likely to help you attain it.

When you have a clear idea in mind of the type of people who will best serve your aims in life, it is your turn to use your Dark NLP techniques to build a connection with them, and get what you want out of them. The first key when attempting this is to learn to adopt the language and way of talking of the type of people you want to attract. For example, if you are attempting to attract a career mentor, you may notice that such people use a particular range of vocabulary, and carry themselves in a certain way. By mirroring these aspects, you can harness the power of NLP to build a deep sense of rapport with these people, and draw them into your life.

Linking yourself with someone's values is another NLP based way of bringing them into your reality. For example, in interacting with someone and reading them using Dark NLP methods found earlier in this book, you may find out that they greatly value freedom. If you can position yourself as someone who represents freedom and who is able to bring more of it into their life, you are helping to ensure that the person will want to be around you. They will be unaware of your manipulative interference and will feel as if they have sought you out entirely of their own accord.

You can use the Dark NLP understanding of power balances to ensure that you remain in control after attracting people into your life. Some of the ways you can ensure you retain power over someone is by using Machiavellian ideas like ensuring they are more reliant on you than you are on them, that you gather more personal information about the person than they are able to find out about you, and that you demonstrate your strength and force of will in a way which intimidates people into complying with you.

Dark NLP teaches that it is important to always reassess your peer group and the amount of time you spend around people. You should always be thinking in terms of if they still benefit your life. Does time you spend with them offer some type of benefit to you in return? Do you still have the balance of power in all of your interactions? By asking these questions on a regular basis, you can ensure that your peer group always exists to serve your needs, and make adjustments to it as needed.

Input = Output

One of the core principles of NLP questions if the influences we take in have a direct influence on our output in life. What does this mean when filtered through the lens of dark psychology? It is our duty and our responsibility to ourselves to ensure that we are only allowing the right influences into our life. While the traditional view of NLP might state that these inputs should be those that promote health and wellbeing, our more ruthless, Dark NLP perspective, teaches us that any input that allows us to shamelessly pursue our desires is one we should permit.

Earlier in this book, we came to understand that time is the only truly valuable resource, as it is the only one we cannot get back. Because of this understanding, we must become incredibly selective in how we spend our time. Most people live their lives on autopilot, passively accepting useless or even harmful influences in the form of television, other people's opinions and information that does not serve a purpose. Dark NLP equips you with the framework of human behavior to understand that we should be very selective about what we permit to enter into our minds.

It is worth seeking out input that directly serves our aims, no matter the supposed morality of the input. For example, if you are in the world of business, you may come across a book which purports to offer you tools and techniques to become more effective. Upon reading further, you may discover the techniques include several which go against the norms of conventional morality. If you were to reject this book on that basis, you would not be thinking according to the tenets of Dark NLP. Your only concern should be with deciding whether the book will offer an input that is useful to pursuing your aims, regardless of the supposed moral goodness of the input.

One of the key tests to subject any input to is whether it empowers you or disempowers you, and whether it teaches you to be active or passive. This stems back to our earlier exploration of the idea that, in any given situation, one party is the predator and one party is the prey. You should proactively seek to ensure that all of the information you are taking in encourages you to take the proactive role of the predator. Anything that seeks to waste our time on passive feelings of security and staying within our comfort zone should be discarded without hesitation. Some common culprits include social media, mainstream music and mainstream radio.

Aim High - Don't Limit Yourself

One of the major mistakes that people make is thinking too small. It is a classic idea found in the world of NLP and self-development that people tend to overestimate the amount of change they can experience in the course of the year, but vastly underestimate the amount they can experience over the course of several years. Similarly, when first finding out about the power of Dark NLP to cause massive amounts of change in their life, people are often too modest about what it is they want. People aim for relatively minor changes instead of the huge, bold changes that Dark NLP is capable of causing. Let's explore some of the reasons for this aiming low.

Perhaps the most common reason for aiming low is a fear of failure. Many of us worry that we are not good enough to achieve what we set out to, and therefore aim low in order to protect ourselves from the pain of failure. Thankfully, there are several ideas from this book which can be used to overcome the fear of failure and stop it from holding us back from making the most out of our potential.

If you have internalized the lessons of this book, you will have come to see that there is no such thing as failure, there is only feedback. You should therefore not hold yourself back from dreaming big and aiming for massive achievements in life. If you do not get there on your first try, there is nothing to be ashamed about. You have simply learned a valuable set of lessons that will help you refine your approach and come closer to your aim at your next attempt.

Another reason to set big goals for ourselves is that even if we fall slightly short, we are likely to have achieved more than if we had set a more modest goal. When you manage to make yourself accept this logical reason to set larger goals, you will begin to feel more comfortable with doing so. A helpful part of this process is learning to reframe fear and nerves as excitement. If you are able to embrace this energy as a positive thing then you can channel it into helping you to attain your aims.

Don't Reinvent the Wheel - Walk the Proven Path

One of the absolute keys to getting what you want out of life, and harnessing the power of Dark NLP in doing so, is finding an appropriate model for any set of goals. This requires you to be open-minded enough to find someone who has achieved what you hope to, and also be non judgmental enough not to pass judgment on the path they have taken to get there. Most of us, often unknowingly, will have a mental idea of the way something should be done. This Dark NLP understanding is informed by the psychological concept of a 'schema' -basically a mental map of the norms of an interaction that should occur.

As we are seeking models of success that we can emulate, we will often find that the way in which people have achieved is very different to the way we expected it to look. For example, within the area of romance, many people have a specific idea of what a woman wants. If their ideas in this area are challenged, it can be difficult to accept that something else actually works. We have to let go of our egos and our pride and remind ourselves that actions should be judged only by the outcomes they produce. If we are close minded enough to reject proven strategies, then we are only harming our own chances of success.

It is not enough to merely seek out someone who has achieved a particular aim you –desire. It is important to try to find someone whose circumstances as closely matched your own as possible. For example, if your aim is to make money, you should try and find someone who had a similar journey to the one that lies ahead of you. It is true that there are lessons that can be learned and applied to a variety of contexts - but success in similar circumstances to your own is more likely to have a wide range of immediately applicable ideas.

When you have found someone whose success you wish to model, whose circumstances seem to be as relevant to your own as possible, it is important to try and summarize their internal and external processes. For example, what was the person's decision making process at the time? What did they focus on? What was the language they used to represent their own subjective appearance to themselves? What external actions did they take? When they experienced setbacks, how did they overcome them? By determining these factors, you develop a model of someone which you can take action on and put into practice for yourself.

Chapter 8 - Understand How to Exploit Your Hidden Advantage

<u>The Constant Predator</u>

With any new system of understanding, and the practical techniques that stem from that outlook, there is a learning curve. You will now be provided with insight into the typical stages of progress that occur when someone is learning Dark NLP for the first time. Each stage of progress will clearly be described and you will be given advice on how to progress to the ultimate aim of Dark NLP - to become a constant predator.

The first stage of learning Dark NLP can be called tentative exploration. In this stage, someone who has heard about this unique perspective on life for the first time begins to consider its ideas and gradually weigh them up against their own perception of the world. At this point, the person does not necessarily agree with the ideas of Dark NLP, or profess them to be true. They are merely judging them in light of their own subjective experience. In order to move beyond this phase, it is advised that you actively seek to apply your understanding of Dark NLP to the world around you. Try and perceive interactions through a Dark NLP lens by looking for aspects such as power struggles and body language communication.

After someone has spent some time trying out the basic ideas behind Dark NLP, and judging if they are a good match with their view of reality, they may eventually begin to agree that Dark NLP at least has the potential to be useful. This stage of the process can be termed cautious acceptance. During this time, you will learn to start to see things through a Dark NLP lens, although to do so will require conscious effort. You will begin to notice that Dark NLP ideas are more apparent to you than they were previously. You may also begin to question your understanding of morality.

In order to push beyond cautious acceptance, you should make a conscious effort to put into practice Dark NLP techniques related to influencing yourself, and influencing others, as quickly as possible. It is only through experiencing personal success in using the techniques that you will begin to accept them fully and feel at ease with their usage in your everyday life.

Following cautious acceptance, you will progress to a level of Dark NLP usage that can be termed casual competence. At this stage, you will begin to naturally think in terms of Dark NLP concepts, and this will require progressively less effort from you. You will also find yourself using Dark NLP to take control of your own life and influence others without having to think about it. The most important distinction that shows you have reached this level of progress is when you realize you are influencing others and you no longer feel guilty about doing so.

In order to make the most of the casual competence stage, it is important that you begin to put into practice the ideas related to tracking the patterns behind your success. You may, for example, at this stage of your progress particularly benefit from keeping a journal as part of an evening routine. You stand the best chance of moving beyond this stage if you are able to identify the difference between the times you succeed and those you do not.

The levels beyond casual competence all involve mastery of Dark NLP to one extent or another. There are no longer so much distinct levels of progress as there are gradual degrees of improvement. Signs that someone has reached the mastery stage of Dark NLP include the ability to read the power balance of any interaction effortlessly and without conscious thought, a clear and constant focus on achieving your outcome in any given situation and the ability to mirror someone else without a second thought and influence them based on a deep, artificial rapport that you create without effort.

Your mastery of Dark NLP is reliant on your willingness to absorb the techniques and concepts described in this book. You must be willing to take massive action within your life and attempt to exert as much influence through the use of Dark NLP as possible. You must always be willing to identify patterns of success that you can model, implement and use to reach the next level of your mastery in the shortest space of time possible.

When you find you think automatically in terms of the core Dark NLP concepts, and you interact with someone in a way that is intended to force rapport with them before exploiting them for your own needs, you have achieved the ultimate aim within Dark NLP, which is to become a constant predator. What exactly does it mean to be a constant predator?

If you have internalized these teachings so far, you will know that reality is always subjective. One of the ways in which this manifests is by allowing people to see themselves as one way in some situations, and another way entirely in others. This can take the form of extreme situational confidence in some environments which evaporates entirely in others. Dark NLP aims to equip you with a detailed understanding of the power balance in any social situational. Its teachings are universal and not reliant on any particular circumstance.

As a result of the situational independence of Dark NLP, when you have fully internalized its techniques you will be able to be effective in any situation. This is because you will be able to generate rapport with anyone you meet, both on a verbal and physical level, and use this skill to take control of any interaction. This will allow you to exhibit confidence and self efficacy regardless of the circumstances in which you are forced to act.

Personal SWOT

One of the most powerful strategic techniques in use within the corporate world is the SWOT framework. This acronym stands for strengths, weaknesses, opportunities and threats. It is intended to provide an insight into the current internal and external positive and negative aspects of a company's strategic position. The framework is useful in identifying both the proactive choices the company needs to make and also the improvements that must be made to reduce identified weaknesses.

The ideas behind the SWOT framework can be adapted and applied at a personal level in order to offer a full insight into an individual's personal strengths, weaknesses and potential next moves at any given time. So how exactly do you conduct a personal SWOT, and how can its information be used?

The first question to ask yourself is to your main strengths and your main weaknesses. You may want to begin my jotting down long lists in no particular order. After you have written down every possible strength and weakness that comes to mind, without judgment, you can begin to narrow them down to five each. Once you have settled on five, you can begin the process of ranking them, in order to determine your own view of your major strengths and weaknesses.

After finding your strengths and weaknesses, aka your view of your inner self, it is important to analyze the range of possible opportunities that exist within your life at the time, and also any possible threats that could disrupt your current way of life.

In order to determine the opportunities you have, it is worth thinking of the possibilities in several areas. Brainstorm the possible moves you could make, or chance occurrences that could happen to you, within the areas of your career, relationships and free time. Don't judge your own thoughts and feel free to write down each and every idea you have. This is important to open your mind to the range of opportunities you could consider pursuing.

You now need to think of all of the things that could disrupt your way of life. For example, is there a chance you could lose your job? Could your romantic relationship come to an end? Could there be a change to your living situation? It is important to think as open-mindedly as possible in order to determine every possible situation to be aware of. It is better to include something that is unlikely than it is to lose your way of life to something you didn't prepare for.

Once you have answered all of the above questions, you will be left with a list of your strengths and weaknesses, as well as the opportunities ahead of you and the threats to your current way of life. It is now time to see if there are areas of overlap between your opportunities and strengths. For example, if there is an opportunity of a new job, do you have any personal strengths that make you suitable for the role? As a general rule, you should prioritize pursuing the opportunities that coincide the best with your strengths.

You must now think of all of your weaknesses in terms of chances for improvement. Let's say, for example, you have identified three primary personal weaknesses - bad presentation skills, low confidence in public speaking and a limited social life. Instead of seeing these as weaknesses, you should see them as puzzles to solve. You may, for example, determine that you can go on a course to improve your presentation skills, join a public speaking club to gain confidence in this area and take up a range of new hobbies in order to broaden your social horizons. You should systematically seek to find solutions to all of your identified weaknesses.

Finally, you should look at the list of threats you have determined to your way of life, and seek ways to protect against them and their impact. For example, if you have determined you are at risk of losing your romantic relationship, you may think of ways to improve your current relationship while also improving your social ability in general, in case you find yourself seeking a new relationship. This example is intended to illustrate the importance of always thinking in two ways - remedying the present and protecting against the future. This dual thought process can be applied to any area of life that is perceived as a threat.

By determining your personal SWOT, you are improving your personal prospects in several major ways. First, you are allowing yourself to find the best fit between the competencies you possess and the options that exist in your external environment. This is a clear advantage over the majority of people who stumble through life, passively taking whichever job or relationship happens to be in front of them at the time. Second, you are taking an honest look at your own areas of weakness and finding actionable, realistic solutions to improve them. Finally, you are considering the major macro, environmental threats that exist, and proactively seeking to prevent them, seeing attack as the best form of defense.

You can use this information to feed into a number of other Dark NLP techniques, such as envisioning your future, influencing others and choosing your habits. For example, as a result of your personal SWOT, you may have identified a strategic match between your strength of intelligence and an opportunity of a master's degree. You could therefore form habits that were in line with attaining this objective, seek out and influence a peer group that would support your ambition and set goals and envision the success of achieving the master's degree. You can see how conducting the personal SWOT exercise will improve your current situation in the short term while also helping you move towards significant goals in the future.

See People through the Sniper Scope

This book has repeatedly emphasized viewing people as operating within their own subjective perception of the world. Everyone makes the decisions that make the most sense at the time. Everyone has a system of hopes, fears, drives and values which directly impact their choices in every area of their life. By understanding someone's personal blueprint, you can cause them to act in a way which serves your own goals and aims. This concept will now be refined to a ruthless level which teaches you to view people through a sniper scope - as targets you must take out in order to reach your goals.

Perhaps the best way to envision the necessary mindset for advanced Dark NLP interpersonal manipulation is as a web. Every individual person in a situation has a place in this web. The connections between people are the strands on the web, representing the power dynamics and the flow of activity between the two people. Every person has an aim and objective and there are probably several other people standing in the way of attaining it.

If you are going to use Dark NLP to manipulate social dynamics to your advantage, it is vital that you always make yourself think in terms of your goal, and identify the people that are standing in your way. When someone is blocking your progress you essentially have three options - passively accept the situation and make no move to advance, seek out a route around the obstacle, or find a way to demolish the obstacle and proceed on your intended path.

Dark NLP offers you the range of techniques you need to take the latter option. There is no need to seek an indirect route around the people that stand in your way, simply gain control of them through Dark NLP and turn them from hindrance to help. You have the option of either building rapport with them and encouraging them to act in a way which hastens your progression, or lowering their self esteem and making them irrelevant to your progress. You can choose to either bring them onto your team, or take them out of the game entirely.

When coming across a new person you must always seek the answers to two questions - how can this person further my aims in life, and what is the most effective way I can gain influence over this person? By asking these questions, you will quickly learn to determine if a person is worth the effort of influencing, by figuring out how they stand to serve you. If they are deemed worthy of influencing, you save yourself time by determining the optimum strategy of doing so.

Breaking Rapport - Potent Enslavement Technique

Up until this point, this book has largely focused on ways you can build rapport with a person in order to soften them up to your influence. You will now be shown how breaking rapport, following a period of building it, is an advanced form of Dark NLP manipulation you can use to drain people's free will and cause them to crave your attention and approval.

Before you can enslave someone through breaking rapport, it is important that you first build a solid level of rapport. This is achieved through the linguistic and physical mirroring processes that are explored in depth earlier in this book. You should reach the stage of influence where you are able to physically pace and lead the body language of the person you are interacting with. When you have achieved this level of rapport, you are ready to begin the process of tactically breaking rapport.

In order to break rapport with someone, stop mirroring them. Stop using the special linguistic markers you have earlier identified. Use a brusque, negative tone of voice and do anything else that gives the opposite of seeking rapport. You will be able to tell when you have achieved this as the person you are interacting with will seem confused or dejected.

When you break a deep level of rapport with someone, you have two immediate effects upon them. First, you cause them to feel a sense of loss, as the good emotions that you were previously triggering have been withdrawn. Second, you trigger the other person's natural inclination to chase and seek your validation to fill the void of your approval. You can use this technique to vary the pace of an interaction and stop it from becoming monotonous or one dimensional.

It is important that after breaking rapport with someone you allow them to regain rapport with you. However, the timing of when you allow this should depend on strategically rewarding some desired statement or behavior. For example, if the person seeking to regain rapport with you touches you, and you wish them to repeat this, you would reconnect rapport with them at that moment. They would subconsciously link the good feelings of rapport with the behavior, and repeat it in the future.

Breaking rapport is a powerful tool and as such should be used sparingly. It is best deployed to introduce an element of tension and chase into an interaction and turbocharge its emotional progress. You can build and break rapport a few times in an interaction, but you should avoid overdoing it. It becomes progressively harder to rebuild deep rapport, and you therefore run the risk of breaking a person's interest in you entirely.

Situational Exploitation Playbook

This following section is the book's most tactical - it involves a series of Dark NLP maneuvers that can be deployed in different situations. For each, the risks and rewards involved are clearly stated, and the concepts involved in each tactic are clearly explained and linked back to sections of the book.

The first type of situation we will explore is related to the professional sphere of life. A range of different career situations will be put forward, along with an actionable understanding of how

Dark NLP can give you an advantage to exploit. You will learn how to use Dark NLP in a job interview, to influence office dynamics, and during a negotiation.

A job interview is one of the most stressful situations you will face. An immense amount of pressure arises from knowing that you are being judged, and as a result of this judgment you will either receive a financially rewarding job, or experience the pain of rejection. A range of applied Dark NLP practices can assist you in the job interview scenario.

One of the most powerful ways Dark NLP can help you before a job interview is by helping you understand your own values and drives. You can take the time to link the potential job to your values and drives as this will ensure your external words and actions and internal beliefs are congruent and aligned. You can also use Dark NLP techniques described earlier to ensure you are able to summon your peak performance state and feeling of deep, primal motivation on command.

In the job interview itself, you can use your understanding of how to build rapport with and influence others to your advantage. You can use your language reading abilities to identify the keywords that have special meaning to your interviewer and subtly use these to sell yourself to them. You can also mirror and influence their body language to check your rapport at any given time. This allows you to answer their questions secure in the knowledge that they are processing your words on a deep level that other candidates would not be able to reach.

Office politics can be a minefield for people who do not understand the true nature of why people behave the way they do. You have shed this conventional outlook and now know how to see people through the lens of Dark NLP to determine their hopes, fears and values. You can apply this knowledge to the workplace.

One workplace application of Dark NLP concepts is to influence the way in which your colleagues perceive each other in relation to their values and fears. For example, you may fear that two colleagues are becoming close and forming an alliance that is not aligned with your own aims. You can use Dark NLP mirroring practices to build rapport with one of the people, and then when they are in a state of greater susceptibility, convince them that the person they had become close to actually contradicted their values and stood for their fears. By influencing the power dynamic of your workplace in this way you can ensure that people respond in the way you need them to without being directly accountable for their views.

One of the most useful applications of Dark NLP within the career aspect of life is in a negotiation. The first thing you should be thinking about when entering a negotiation is finding someone's linguistic blueprint. This will enable you to tell what they are really thinking at any stage of the negotiation, and how to manipulate it accordingly.

Your next major concern should be to use subtle aspects of physical mirroring to increase the sense of rapport with the person you are negotiating with. You should note that it is difficult to conduct a full mirroring within the context of a negotiation - doing so may seem too obvious and draw too much attention. Instead, you should focus on mirroring particular aspects of their physicality.

You can also use a toned down variation of the breaking rapport concept in the course of your negotiation. You shouldn't fully break rapport by combining physical and verbal breaking rapport tactics, but you can, for example, lessen rapport by switching up your tone of voice, or ceasing to mirror something physical. This should be done after a point in the negotiation you wish to discourage. In the period following your breaking of rapport, the other party will be more likely to agree to concessions. Use this wisely at a time when you need to secure some form of agreement as part of the negotiation.

Dark NLP also gives you the means to succeed within the area of romantic relationships. For example, you may have the sticking point that, on dates, you are unable to build a sense of connection with the person you are dating. Dark NLP offers you two easy to use tools to fix this problem - verbal and physical mirroring.

Your first move in this situation should be to get the person talking about something positive, and to keenly note any special or unusual words they use to describe what they are saying. If, for example, their physicality changes when they say a certain word, such as their eyes widening, this is a sign that the word is loaded with additional, personal, emotional meaning.

When you wish to encourage a sense of agreement and warmth between you and your date, you can use their special word. You should not draw attention to the fact you are using it, or make it stand out in any way. You want it to seem as smooth and natural as possible. Your date's conscious mind will not pick up on the fact of what you have done. On a deeper level, however, they will feel a sense of connection with you they would not have experienced if you used a different word.

You can also adapt your choice of language to reflect the person you are dating's values. For example, over the course of an interaction, you may notice that the person values expression and creativity. You can then use a lot of language that ties into these values. For example, you may use words like unstifled, imagination, externalize and other language that you feel will connect with them on a values based level.

By using language that evokes your date's deepest values, they will feel as if you are 'their kind of person.' They are likely to feel a deep sense of connection with you, and will often express sentiments such as the feeling of having known you a long time, when they have not. The best part of all about this technique is there is no way at all of linking the feeling of rapport into your choice of language. It is a very subtle and hard to detect, but profoundly powerful, way of romantically influencing someone.

Chapter 9 - Powerful Dark Hypnotic Seduction

In this chapter you will be given a complete guide to putting the principles of Dark NLP into action in your pursuit of romantic success. No matter what your particular romantic goals happen to be, this chapter will give you a personal blueprint to achieving them. You will learn the internal and external aspects of seducing someone using dark hypnotic ideas. By the end of this chapter, you will have a full range of beliefs, theories and tactics that can be used to take hypnotic romantic control over somebody. You can use this either as a warning or as inspiration - the choice is yours.

Kill Your Limiting Beliefs

The first thing that needs to take place in order for you to have the potential of succeeding at using Dark NLP romantically is to systematically eliminate your limiting beliefs. There are a number of widely reoccuring limiting beliefs specifically related to romantic seduction. We will now show you ways of overcoming the most common doubts and fears you will encounter. This will clear the path for you to achieve success through seduction based on Dark NLP.

The most common limiting belief is that using Dark NLP ideas to seduce someone is somehow immoral or wrong. This limiting belief stems from two major sources - a view of seduction as 'it should be a certain way' and a misunderstanding of exactly what Dark NLP seduction entails.

People often believe that seduction should look a certain way because they have gained an understanding of attraction that is based on books and movies, rather than on firsthand experience. This leads people to believe that things that make for good movie scenes accurately represent the process of one person becoming attracted to another. As a result, when they see something that disagrees with their preconceptions, such as hypnotic seduction, they reject it.

Some people are also against hypnotic seduction on the basis that it somehow removes the element of choice from a person and makes them do things they don't want to do. This couldn't be further from the truth. Hypnotic seduction simply teaches you how to connect with someone on a profoundly deep level and how to trigger good emotions in them that they associate with you. They still have the freedom of choice - you are simply greatly influencing your chances by your ability to give the other person a good experience and connect with you far faster than normal.

Some people are worried that they will not be able to understand or put into practice the techniques needed for romantic uses of Dark NLP. This logical sounding objection is usually used to mask something deeper, such as a fear of connecting with other people or some personal insecurity. The deeper insecurities are overcome by a willingness to put the ideas and process of this chapter into action. The worry that the process will be too hard is understandable but unfounded. The ideas in this chapter are simple and actionable by anybody.

The Theory of Romantic Seduction

There are several theoretical foundations that underpin the rest of this chapter. These ideas aim to explain why the principles of Dark NLP are so effective in seducing others. This section can be thought of as the 'why' behind hypnotic seduction, while later chapters are the 'how'. It is important to note that your ability to use the techniques effectively will depend largely upon how well you understand why they work. For this reason, it is important to pay close attention to this section, and internalize its ideas.

The first idea which is key to your understanding of hypnotic seduction is the idea that people inherently seek out others they feel comfortable and secure around. Usually, this happens over a prolonged period of time, as the result of two people going through a range of shared experiences together. Using the ideas of Dark NLP, however, it is possible to artificially speed up this sense of shared experience and allow people to connect quicker than would otherwise be possible.

The second main principle behind using Dark NLP in pursuit of seduction is that people aim to find others who share the same values as they do. This is usually a hit and miss affair that takes a long period of time since someone's deepest values do not easily arise in the course of a natural interaction. Using Dark NLP, however, it is possible to elicit someone's values quickly and then subtly embed them into your choice of language and the stories you tell. The means of doing this is explained in full later in the chapter.

Next, you must come to understand that people are less fully in control of their own actions than they realize. By reading their actions and language choices we can influence them on a deep level. It is usually the case of presenting the strongest reality relative to the person you are aiming to seduce.

With the above principles in mind, the skilled hypnotic seducer is able to deploy a range of techniques, tailor made for various stages of the romantic interaction. They always know exactly what to say and are always able to advance the emotional progression of the interaction within a shorter than expected length of time.

The Controversy of the Techniques

There have been some high-profile teachers of hypnotic seduction who have attracted more than their share of controversy. We will now explore some of the reasons why the hypnotic seduction techniques detailed in this chapter are so controversial. A response to the controversy will be put forward in order to present a more balanced viewpoint of the issue. The reader is then free to form their own opinion based on the facts presented to them.

One of the most common criticisms of hypnotic seduction and those who teach it is that the techniques force people into doing things they otherwise wouldn't. Part of the reason why this controversy is so often related with hypnotic seduction is due to the way that the major teachers market their ideas and products. Some of the marketing language associated with the products sometimes wrongly describes the purpose of the techniques. This can lead to a controversy over the forcing of people to do things - a criticism that does not correspond with the actual teachings of hypnotic seduction.

Another controversy involving the teachings in this chapter is that they teach men to be dissatisfied with their love lives and to commit infidelity. The theory goes that if men become aware of the potential to use powerful Dark NLP principles to attract a greater variety of the women they desire, then they will be less willing to settle down into a committed relationship. In actual fact, this is far from how things usually transpire.

It is often the lack of choice and the desire to have the possibility of a relationship that drives people to consider hypnotic seduction techniques. It is wrong to assume that people using these techniques are looking for something other than the traditional relationship ideal. Although some people are, the majority are looking to use the techniques to find someone suitable to have a conventional relationship with.

Some people have criticized this method of seduction for teaching people to hide who they really are and instead rely on tricks and techniques. This is a misconception, as the remainder of this chapter will show. The techniques do not require someone to hide who they are; instead, they require you to refine and enhance who you are in order to present the best version of yourself to people.

Creating the Hypnotic Mood

The first key to achieving success in the field of seduction using Dark NLP is to create an appropriate mood. There are several factors which contribute to the ideal mood within which to use Dark NLP. Ideally, there should not be any form of background noise which is distracting from the content of the conversation. There should, however, be some form of background noise to ensure that there are no awkward silences.

In addition to making sure the levels of background noise are just right, it is important to make sure you are in an environment where you are unlikely to be disturbed. This does not necessarily mean you cannot interact in public. It is possible to carry out these techniques in a public environment such as a nightclub or bar. The key is choosing a spot within the location that minimizes your chance of being interrupted by other people.

The surroundings should feel informal and relaxed if possible. This is intended to ensure both you and the person you are interacting with feel relaxed and open enough to communicate deeply with one another. If the atmosphere feels too constrained or formal then it can inhibit the ability to create a sufficient level of intimacy for romance to occur.

The ideal atmosphere will also be one in which physical contact, such as kissing, can occur. This should be an area where physicality can occur without others judging. Dark NLP teaches that people are reliant on their drives and values as influences of their behavior. Many people have the value of behaving a certain way in public through fear of being judged. It is your job as a user of Dark NLP to take this value into account and find a location where no judgment will occur.

Seductive Anchoring

The NLP concept of anchoring is one of the most powerful tools you can use in your pursuit of seduction. What exactly is meant by seductive anchoring, and what does it allow you to do? Simply put, seductive anchoring involves helping people to feel deep feelings of positive emotion. They then have these feelings tied directly to you, so being around you is an immediate trigger for good feelings. This allows you to always be a source of positive emotion for that person and become a valuable part of their life.

So how exactly does the process of seductive anchoring take place? The first step is to ensure that the frame between yourself and the person you are interacting with is romantic. You both need to be aware of the fact that your time spent together signifies something more serious than friendship. Otherwise, your anchoring efforts will result in a deepening of a friendship connection, as opposed to deepening the sense of romance between you.

When you are interacting with someone romantically, you should guide them into a state of strong positive emotion. You can achieve this by asking a series of questions and asking the person to recall some of their fondest memories. It is important that you get them to elaborate upon the topic and ask about it in detail. Every time you ask a question that will elicit a positive feeling, you should perform some subtle, repeated gestures, such as touching your wrist.

By repeating a physical gesture while invoking a positive emotion, you will link the physical stimulus with the emotion in the person's mind. After you repeat this a sufficient number of times, you will find that you are able to invoke the positive feeling in the person simply by carrying out the physical stimulus. There will be no need for you to logically guide them to the emotional state again because eventually they will experience the emotions and not be able to pinpoint logically why they are happening. This means that there is no risk of your techniques being discovered as they are too subtle to be picked up on.

You should always use seductive anchoring as a way of ensuring the person you are interacting with feels good around you and is comfortable. It is important to realize that you can only do this congruently if deep down you have good intentions for the person. If you are acting in a way which is intending to promote comfort, but deep down you do not have good intentions, you will give off an incongruent vibe and lose your influence. Dark NLP teaches that being aligned in our thoughts, words and actions is essential to exerting influence.

It is important to understand that seductive anchoring should be used to enhance an existing romantic interaction, not as the entire basis for one. Some people, when realizing the power of the technique, make the mistake of thinking it can form the foundation of a romantic encounter. This is a mistake. There needs to be something of substance between the person you are interacting with and yourself, a genuine chemistry, or at least the appearance of it. Seductive anchoring can enhance a connection between people but it cannot create one on its own.

Us vs. Them

One of the key ideas that makes Dark NLP unique is its ability to translate psychological findings into actionable steps. One such actionable step relates to creating a sense of connection and intimacy during the course of seduction. This technique is intended to create a shortcut to the feeling of sharing a secret, special relationship with someone that is usually only possible after spending a lot of time together.

One of the main reasons why our long term friendships feel so special and important to us is because we feel we have a shared set of references, of in jokes and secret language with these people that we don't have with people we know less well. Dark NLP offers several techniques that can be used to make this happen with someone new in a short space of time. To begin with, you should create inside jokes with the person you are trying to seduce. This could be a silly nickname for them, a word for something that happens or something else that only the pair of you understand.

Whenever possible, you should use a technique called 'callback humor' to deepen the sense of Us vs. Them that the previous section described. Once you have determined a few unique names and sayings that show you have a special connection with the person you wish to seduce, you should make reference to them in the future at appropriate times. By recalling these phrases, you create a special sense of shared history and humor that makes the person feel a disproportionate amount of comfort around you in relation to the time they have known you.

You can deepen this sense of Us vs. Them by emphasizing the commonalities between yourself and the person you are trying to become romantic with. If, for example, you order the same drink when you are out, you can use this small detail as the basis for a funny story about how ordering this drink shows you both have exquisite taste and aren't like the rest of the people in the bar. Even seemingly minor and unimportant commonalities can be used as the basis for making quirky and unique connections. You should be aware of which connections your person of interest responds well to. You should keep and refer back to the ones that get a positive response, and stop referring to the ones which get a less positive reception.

Embedded Stories
Embedded stories are a way of conveying that you share deep, meaningful values with someone

that you are trying to pursue romantically. The concept of embedded stories draws upon an idea within the world of romance known as 'tribe theory.' This theory states that when seeking out a romantic partner, people look for someone who is either in the same social 'tribe' as themselves, is in a superior tribe to theirs or is in an equal but different tribe that the person is interested in experiencing.

This theory, when combined with the Dark NLP understanding of human nature, states that people will have a different series of values for each of the three tribes. For example, the values of their own tribe will be those that the person personally holds and are in conjunction with the general social expectation for someone of their standing. The values of the tribe superior to theirs are often values they aspire to holding in the future. Finally, the values of the interesting tribe are often those which the person feels attracted to but feels are taboo for reasons of social pressure.

The first step in using this theory of tribes and their values to your advantage in romantic seduction is figuring out which tribe you will portray yourself as being in. The method for this is as follows. If you genuinely share a lot in common with the object of your affection, it is best to portray yourself as being in the same tribe as them. If there is something about you which puts you in higher standing than the person you are seeking to seduce, such as you are better educated, then it is best to portray yourself as being in the superior tribe. If you have a personality trait which is exotic to the person you are aiming to seduce, such as being particularly carefree and adventurous, then you may wish to portray yourself as being from the interesting but different tribe.

Once you have settled upon a tribal identity that you will convey during the course of the seduction, it is important to settle upon the values that the person is likely to associate with your chosen tribe. For example, if you are portraying yourself as being from the superior tribe, which values does this person aspire to?

Having a clear understanding of the values you wish to convey is essential to being able to effectively embed them into stories.

The main purpose of an effective embedded value story is to convey a certain compatibility with a person while occupying their logical mind with an engaging story. The aspects that convey the value are hidden and not the primary focus of the story. Instead, they are subtly woven into it through sub-communications, choice of language and the subtext of the story.

We will now look at some practical examples of how values can be embedded into stories. Let's imagine that you had chosen to portray yourself as being from the same tribe as the object of your interest and one of the values you had identified was reliability. You might tell a story which, on the surface, seems to be about a trip you took while on vacation. It should be interesting enough to keep the attention of the person you are telling it to. However, the language you use should subtly relate to reliability such as phrases like "Things worked out as planned," "I never let people down," "The car was reliable," "I chose them because they offer a reliable service" and any other way you can allude to the theme.

The benefits of telling an embedded story is that it allows you to associate a value with yourself that is not questioned by the person's logical mind. Because you distract them with the linear story they accept your value allusions at a deeper level. This allows you to influence their perception of you and their standing in relation to you. By choosing values that you feel will give you a greater chance of seducing the person, you achieve a lot more through your conversation than most people's small talk is ever able to.

Signature Touches and Gestures

The preceding section of this chapter explained how you can map out a person's desired values and subtly associate yourself with those values. This has the basic purpose of making you stand out in the other person's mind as someone unique, valuable and worthy of attention. Another way in which you can further this perception is by making use of signature touches and gestures. This is a Dark NLP drawing upon the teachings of charismatic psychology.

Some of the most memorable speakers in history are known for making certain gestures or motions when they speak. In order for you to come across as more charismatic, and therefore more influential, you can deploy a range of specific motions when you speak. It is important that the gestures match the tone of your words. For example, if you are talking about opening up, you should perform an open gesture. This will ensure your actions and words are congruently aligned.

If you sparingly use a few signature motions and gestures, which you deploy consistently to coincide with a certain function of your speech, then you will stand out in the other person's mind as charismatic and memorable. Only a small part of the meaning we convey to someone is associated with our words. Far more is through aspects such as our tone and body language. By using repeated gestures and motions we are able to convey a greater level of meaning to our words and also condition the person we are interacting with to respond to us consistently when triggered by the gesture.

When you feel you have a sufficient level of connection and comfort with someone, you can begin the possibility of exploring some subtle way of touching them that you repeat and use as a form of anchoring. Say, for example, you are consistently able to make the object of your romantic affection laugh by making a certain reference or telling a certain type of joke. If, at the moment they laugh, you touch them on the same part of their arm, then they will begin to associate the positive emotion of laughter and happiness with your touch. You can then trigger this feeling in them, even without the stimulus of humor, by repeating the touch.

When using techniques such as the touch, you should be careful not to overuse them. They work because they are under the radar and are not consciously understood. Because of this, they do not trigger the usual rational thought processes and defense mechanisms that people have when interacting. If, however, you overuse the touches then people will register what you are doing. They will automatically put their guard up and your level of influence will diminish.

Chapter 10 - Learn from the Masters of NLP

Powerful Wisdom, Condensed

By this point in the book you have a detailed understanding of not only the theory and framework behind Dark NLP but also how to apply the techniques to get what you want and need out of life. One of the key concepts of Dark NLP is not learning how to do something through trial and error, but instead seeking out someone who has already made the mistakes for you, and following their footsteps to success.

With this principle of seeking out greatness in mind, you will now be given three insights into the various ways that ideas from NLP can be applied. The three people who have been chosen for this chapter show the various uses for NLP. They all share a common ability to take the principles and techniques of NLP and use them in a certain area of life in a way that is able to capture the imagination of the public at the same time.

For each of the three figures, you will be given some key insights into exactly what has led their understanding of NLP to become so influential within their chosen field. You will have the key concepts they teach distilled and summarized in a way which makes them easy to grasp. In addition to factual information about the people and what they teach, you will be given a succinct summary of the main ways they can be modeled. Their outlooks in life, and the ways they can be applied for your benefit, will be carefully detailed.

Ross Jeffries

Ross Jeffries is one of the most notorious and divisive names within the world of NLP. He is infamous for taking the concepts of NLP and applying them to the world of seduction. Jeffries is said to be the basis for various Hollywood characters exhibiting behaviors of this cocky, self-assured guru. Jeffries is loathed by many for using shock value marketing techniques to draw negative attention to NLP. He is considered by some to condone unacceptable ideas such as not taking into account the level of consent and permission that is present in an interaction.

Jeffries is also known for having a series of high profile disagreements and feuds with former students. A common theme to these controversies is Jeffries feeling as if he has somehow been unfairly treated. In landmark book of seduction *The Game*, author Neil Strauss detailed how Jeffries was bitter whenever another teacher disagreed with his understanding of seduction.

Ross Jeffries has been featured in a number of high profile television documentaries. In these, he has been able to showcase the power of his applications of NLP, including his ability to seductively anchor deeply powerful positive feelings to himself in a short space of time.

Their Unique Take

Perhaps the key contribution of Ross Jeffries to the world of NLP is his ability to take the principles and techniques in general and refine them for a specific purpose. While many users of NLP had long been aware of their potential to enhance romantic interactions, Jeffries was the first to formalize a system. In doing so, Jeffries paved the way for many later teachers who would adapt the concepts of NLP into their own formal method of study.

Jeffries was also one of the first high profile NLP teacher to tap into the potential of marketing NLP in a way which suggests it almost gives its users superpowers. Jeffries was able to suggest that taking one of his seminars or buying one of his products would enable the purchaser to exercise a godlike level of control over other people. While it is true that NLP does greatly enhance the levels of influence a person experiences, Jeffries made it sound like something unimaginably profound.

One of the legacies of Jeffries within the world of NLP is his contribution to the use of in-depth, technical jargon to refer to different concepts. He uses a variety of unique words to describe everyday activities. For example, meeting members of the opposite sex is known as 'sarging.' Ironically, Jeffries use of this type of language is an example of NLP concepts being used against its own customers. Jeffries is fostering a sense of 'Us vs. Them' in which the chosen insiders understand the secret language that is spoken. In order to continue this positive feeling of being on the inside, people are willing to continue spending money on products and seminars.

The Lessons

The lessons that can be learned from Ross Jeffries mainly revolve around the power of applying NLP in a concentrated area of life. In the case of Jeffries, he showed that existing techniques could be modified and used to seduce people. You can take this idea of modified application and apply it to almost any area. For example, imagine you work in sales. You can ask yourself questions such as "How can this technique be used to help close a sale? "and "How do the ideas behind NLP relate to the ideas behind sales?" By seeking commonalities between NLP and a specific area of life you will devise unique and effective applications of its concepts.

We can also learn from Jeffries the importance of expressing our ideas in a memorable and attention grabbing way. The genius of Jeffries was not in inventing new ideas - it was presenting existing ideas in a way which was understandable and easy to remember. When we are trying to explain our ideas to someone we should be sure to summarize them and use techniques such as alliteration and emotional language to increase the chances of being recalled later. If you are able to come across as charismatic then you are more likely to have your words remembered.

Tony Robbins

Tony Robbins is one of the most well-known and recognizable teachers of motivation and self-improvement techniques in the world. He is known for his series of books, audio products and seminars which help people to take control of their lives and find ways to tap into their states of peak performance and creativity.

Ever since Tony Robbins' earliest book, he has made direct reference to the power of NLP to achieve rapid results. Robbins is an advocate of NLP to help people realize what they want out of life, motivate themselves to take action and to stay motivated along their journey. Robbins draws upon both the broad concepts underpinning NLP, as well as specific techniques found within it, to help people unlock their potential in life.

Their Unique Take

Robbins' unique take on NLP was the ability to combine it with other related concepts to enhance its power and appeal. For example, Robbins was able to combine ideas such as NLP visualizations with methods drawn from literature related to time management and goal setting to give people a system that was more powerful than any of its component parts.

Robbins was also able to directly link the benefits of using NLP with his own techniques and teachings. Often, people are turned off from NLP because the people explaining it focus too heavily on the process itself and the concepts behind it, rather than conveying the benefits a person will experience as a result of using NLP. Robbins was able to convince people to buy into what he was teaching as he sold them on how it would improve their life in the process.

Robbins was also able to build trust in himself and his methods by presenting an impressive track record. No matter which stage of his career Robbins was at, he was able to refer to his past achievements in a way which made his words sound credible. For example, in his earliest book, Robbins was able to talk about using NLP to help a large number of patients overcome their addictions and phobias in a far shorter space of time than traditional therapy would allow. In his next book, Robbins was able to refer to the millions of people helped by his first book, and so forth. No matter how famous Robbins was, he was able to make a positive and convincing example from his past.

Robbins was also one of the most prominent mainstream teachers of using the NLP understanding of values for personal motivation. Robbins made the connection between understanding our values and tying them into our everyday activities to lend them greater meaning and significance. Robbins had observed in his years of practice that people were more inclined to stick with a course of action if they felt it was in harmony with their wider view of the world and what mattered in it.

Robbins also had the ability to present NLP as one tool in a wider, holistic approach to self-improvement and management. He presented the teachings of NLP as existing in harmony with other aspects of self improvement such as health and fitness, nutrition and memory retention. In doing this, Robbins was able to make NLP seem more acceptable to a wider number of people. By presenting NLP as one tool of many, rather than the 'one true path', Robbins removed any suspicion of NLP as being dogmatic or somehow cult-like.

The Lessons

A number of lessons can be drawn from the example of Tony Robbins. First, we can use his model to understand how NLP fits in with the other activities in our life. For example, we might hold strong opinions on social policy and the way in which a society should act. How does our understanding of Dark NLP support or challenge these notions? Do we gain a greater insight into another aspect of life through our usage of Dark NLP?

Robbins also teaches people to constantly keep in mind the need to look beyond the apparent meaning of words and events. This is in harmony with the Dark NLP teaching that it is not the apparent surface meaning of things that matters; instead, it is the personal meaning that people assign to them. This manifests in the Dark NLP practices of always striving to ensure you understand what a person means when they use a given word, and remembering to take everyone as a unique individual, rather than making behavioral assumptions based on the behavior of other people.

Robbins also makes clear the need to have both motivation and strategy in order to achieve our aims in life. It is not enough to only feel motivated because motivation is short-lived and will wear off. If all we have is our motivation, then our efforts are likely to be inconsistent and our goals elusive. It is important to combine the temporary ups and downs of motivation with something more substantial - a tried and tested strategy of how to achieve our goals, that has been carefully modeled from someone who has succeeded in similar circumstances to ours.

We can also learn from Robbins how NLP can be used to inspire and energize mass audiences at one time. Robbins is known for embedding his seminars with NLP language that is used to excite and enthuse those watching him. NLP is often emphasized as something that can be used to motivate ourselves or small number of people at once. Robbins helps inspire us to realize that we can use the ideas of NLP to make a difference to large numbers of people at once.

Derren Brown

Derren Brown is an entertainer who uses a blend of NLP and psychology to achieve amazing feats of influence over people. In many ways, Brown uses something close to modern Dark NLP as he combines insights into the unknown aspects of the human psyche with the tactics and concepts of NLP to achieve potent results.

Brown's defining feature is his ability to make people carry out behaviors and do things that seem genuinely inexplicable and amazing. Occasionally, one of Brown's television specials or books will offer a rare insight into the combination of techniques and ideas that make up his work. What most of his abilities have in common is their usage of the nuances of human behavior and perception to be manipulated for a particular purpose.

Their Unique Take

One of the reasons that Brown stands out from other entertainers is his ability to take a single principle from NLP or psychology and make it into an amazing and entertaining visual spectacle. For example, Brown wished to show people the power of using embedded orders and commands, a Dark NLP tactic, to make people do extraordinary things.

Brown was filmed visiting a series of shops in New York City with blank pieces of paper in the shape of bank notes. When entering into a dialogue with the shop worker, Brown would keep their logical mind occupied by telling some seemingly mundane story. When it came time to pay, Brown would subliminally issue the command "Take it, it's fine" within the confines of the story. For example, he may have been telling a story about his reluctance to catch the subway. By using the embedded order, he influences the shop worker to accept the blank paper.

Brown has also found numerous ways to combine the ideas of NLP with the principles of showmanship and stage magic. He will often take an idea from NLP, such as its techniques of helping people to have strong visualizations based on rich sensory data. Brown applied this particular idea to make a volunteer perceive their own senses as if they were a wooden dummy. Brown is doing nothing more than carrying out the NLP techniques, but in a way which is captivating to an audience.

The Lessons

Several ideas can be applied from Derren Brown into a more everyday practice of Dark NLP. First, Brown shows us that people are very suggestible, and are vulnerable to hidden commands. If you are able to disguise commanding language into a seeming innocuous phrase, you stand a chance of causing people to behave a certain way despite never knowing why.

Brown also teaches us to find innovative ways of applying psychological theories. For example, you might read about a particular psychological principle, such as the tendency of people to go along with a majority influence. Instead of simply thinking of this as an interesting fact you have read, you should devise a way to leverage it to your benefit. For example, you might conspire with a group of friends to influence a third party to make a bet you are sure to win. Brown teaches us that for every psychological finding, there is a unique and interesting way of applying it to the real world.

We can also take from Brown the potential to combine NLP with other techniques of influence for even greater effect. For example, Brown combines NLP with sleight of hand to produce some unique and interesting illusions. We can combine NLP ourselves with other skills we have, such as comedy, or public speaking. By drawing upon the unique strengths of NLP, but adding to them with competencies found outside of NLP, we are able to find powerful new uses for its principles.

Chapter 11 - Inaction Equals Death

<u>You Are The 1%</u>

You now have the complete picture of Dark NLP and its immense power to affect change in every area of your life. You know exactly what Dark NLP is and how it combines the most impactful aspects of NLP and psychology into a unique system of influence. You know how to take control of yourself first before extending your influence over those around you.

You have been blessed with the opportunity to create the life of your deepest desires. Dark NLP allows you to explore exactly what you crave from life, free of the worry of social pressure, or a pressure to want certain things. You now know how to free yourself of all doubt and all judgment and just go after what you want in life.

The level of choice and understanding of how the world really works makes you a rare breed. You are truly the 1%. You are one of the few who realize that life is what we make it and we have within our grasp the ability to model the success of any other human being and achieve the same results they have.

Getting Started is the Hardest Part

Many people, when grasping the power of Dark NLP for the first time, experience an ironic feeling of paralysis. They realize that life is now so rich, so abundant with possibility that they feel intimidated and unsure of exactly how to go about making use of their new freedom.

You need to realize that taking the first step is the hardest part of your journey. When you get going, you build up momentum which will carry you forward. Starting out though, you have no inherent momentum. It is up to you to make use of the tools and ideas you now have to energize and enthuse yourself into taking action.

The best way of getting started is to think of one small step you can take to make a little progress in every major area of life. For example, you may want to get your health handled. To do this, you know you will have to join a gym and exercise regularly. This may seem to be a big task. You can see it as simply, however, as taking the first step of finding out the price of a gym to join. By taking even this first small step, you will create invaluable momentum that will propel you along a path of action towards achieving your goals.

Dream Big

There are many things in life that will try and hold us back and limit the scope of ambition. Ironically, few limitations are as damaging to us as the ones we place on ourselves. Don't let the ways in which you use this book be held back by doubt or a lack of self belief. Truly and deeply understand that that there is no limit to your potential. Ordinary people achieve extraordinary things all the time, and will continue to do so. Freeing yourself from your own limitations is the crucial first step in achieving big things in life.

Live by Your Own Code

The techniques and ideas in this book inevitably raise some ethical questions. While reading this book's contents, it is likely that certain sections will have made you more uncomfortable than others. Interestingly, different people react badly to different parts. Some people are most uncomfortable about the idea of dreaming big and setting huge goals in their lives. Other people are more worried about having to exert influence over others.

What is important is you devise your own code of ethics and live by it. Find out exactly how you feel about the different tactics and concepts in this book and see where your comfort level rests. You can always refine and adapt your code of ethics along your journey. It is important to have one at all times, however. Without a set of ethics, you will not know what is and is not acceptable. Your usage of Dark NLP is intended to be liberating and empowering. Using it in a guilt free way is a cornerstone of this experience.

Shape the World as You See Fit

Perhaps the core message of Dark NLP is that you are in the driving seat. You do not passively have to accept what you are given in life. You can figure out the processes behind people and things and then use them to your own advantage.

The ultimate implication of this power is that you can exert influence on the world around you. You can lead people and situations to better reflect your ideals. If you think that people should exhibit more of a certain behavior or value, it is within your grasp to push them in that direction.

In order to fulfill the potential of this influence, you need to have a clear idea of what you want to achieve. An overall strategy or approach to life will ensure you make consistent, principled decisions and end up having an impact on the world around you that you are happy with.

It is not the role of this book to judge the vision you have. Whatever you desire to make the world into is entirely up to you. You owe it to yourself that your vision is entirely yours; however, it should not be shaped by external influences.

So what do you want out of life? No matter what it is, you have run out of excuses not to get it. Every second counts now. Every second you spend not taking action is a second wasted. When you have knowledge this powerful, why not use it?

Seize the day. Make the world your own. Begin. Now.

Other books available by author on Kindle, paperback and audio

Dark Psychology 101: Learn The Secrets Of Covert Emotional Manipulation, Dark Persuasion, Undetected Mind Control, Mind Games, Deception, Hypnotism, Brainwashing And Other Tricks Of The Trade

Printed in Great Britain
by Amazon